WORKING AT HOME

Lindsey O'Connor

HARVEST HOUSE PUBLISHERS
Eugene, Oregon 97402

WORKING AT HOME: A DREAM THAT'S BECOMING A TREND

Copyright © 1990 by Harvest House Publishers
Eugene, Oregon 97402

Library of Congress Cataloging-in-Publication Data

O'Connor, Lindsey, 1961-
    Working at home: a dream that's becoming a trend / Lindsey
    O'Connor.
    ISBN 0-89081-799-5
    1. Home-based businesses   I. Title.
HD2333.033   1990   89-24751
658'.041—dc20   CIP

Printed in the United States of America.

This book is lovingly dedicated to the three biggest reasons I work at home: Jacquelyn, Claire, and Collin. And to Tim, for giving me the inspiration that day at our kitchen table to start a home business.

CONTENTS

ACKNOWLEDGMENTS

Tim, thanks for pitching in with more than your fair share of dishes, diapers, and deadlines, and for being my CPA and tax adviser. God bless you for being the head of our home, and for believing in my dreams!

Paul and Earlene, my parents, thanks for your encouragement and support. You're always there when I need you.

Brenda, thanks for being the catalyst to spark this book. Your touch has added *so* much.

Mom O., thanks for your help while I worked on this manuscript.

Karen, you are my home-business mentor. Thank you for the inspiration and advice.

Ida, without you our business would certainly overtake our home. Thanks for all the things you do for us. You're a part of our family.

Donna, Nancy, and Mary, thanks for pitching in and making my load lighter when things got a little complicated.

Thanks to all of the home-business owners who so candidly shared their stories in this book for the benefit of others who desire to work at home.

Thanks to the staff at Harvest House for supporting this project.

And most of all, thank You, Lord, for "establishing my plans" and "daily bearing my burdens."

So You Want to Work at Home . . .

September 18, 1984

"It's funny the mixed feelings a person can have over extremely important matters in life. My baby is three months old and I just love being a mom. The work is never done, but she is such a blessing that she makes up for the hard times. However, lately I've been thinking about my old job. The thought of getting back into the grind is not at all appealing, but the work itself is. So is the money, since things are a little tight these days. I miss using my skills, but I don't want to leave my baby. What I'd love to do is work out of my home. Perhaps the Lord will show me something."

He did. I started my own home business, as have millions of others. While working on this book, I was astounded by the response from people all over the country who were successfully working at home. Others clamored for more information about how they could do the same thing.

Now it seems like everywhere I go, I run into people who are home-based. Some are women wanting the privilege of raising their own children. Others are men who have given up the corporate rat race. More than a few are building successful careers and creating tremendously profitable businesses. Many are nurturing a part-time solution to their financial problems. And some, as one home-worker put it, just want to be able to cut million-dollar deals over the phone while wearing their pajamas and bunny slippers. Whatever the reasons, working at home is a trend on the rise.

This book was born out of a desire to give other people the encouragement, motivation, and tools necessary to be able to work at home. My prayer is that our families might be strengthened through a reevaluation of the way in which we work.

—Lindsey O'Connor

1
A Dream That's Becoming a Trend

I turned my computer off and closed up shop for the day to go and pick up my children, who were playing at a friend's house. When I got there my friend's little boy asked me what I had been doing. I replied, "I'm writing a book about working at home the way your mommy and I do." He answered simply, "Sounds good." But the father, overhearing my comment, chirped, "Oh, so it's going to be a comedy?"

Working at home definitely has its humorous moments. It can be a tremendous joy, and sometimes it can get crazy enough that you just have to laugh at yourself. But whether you're laughing or not, one thing is certain: Working at home is the dream that more and more people are making a reality.

Forget the commute, skip the office protocol, and don't even think about full-time daycare. Perhaps you've been thinking about various ways to earn an income without working outside your home. Maybe you've been racking your brain to think of a way to provide a living or supplement your income without having to put your children in full-time daycare. Or possibly you're just tired of working for someone else. If you've considered a home business for any reason, you're not alone.

Nancy, Gary, Barbara, Brian, and Heidi are five people who have different reasons for working from their homes. Perhaps you can identify with one of them.

Nancy is a certified public accountant who quit her traditional office job to stay home with her children when number two came along. She wants to raise her own children, but until her husband's business grows a little more, she needs to help with the income. She decided to start a small, part-time bookkeeping business in her home. "It's important for me to be able to stay home with our kids. I would love to be a full-time mom, but right now I have to help supplement our income. I'm hoping to get some computer equipment soon so that I can continue to add clients. Even though I really only want a part-time business, I enjoy keeping my accounting skills fresh while I'm home with my children."

Gary worked at various jobs to support his wife and two children before he started his advertising agency in his home. Even though he wants it to continue to grow financially, he says he will always be home-based. After working the nine-to-five routine for so long, he loves the fact that going to work now means just going across the hall. "I feel sorry for all those people who have to get up and go somewhere every day. Whenever I have early-morning meetings and am forced to join the other rush-hour commuters, I wonder how people can spend an hour or two on the road every day commuting. To own a business and be locked in traffic is the most frustrating thing in the world—even with a car phone. Working at home is great. People who call don't know whether I have 20 employees and am wearing a tie or not!"

Barbara is committed to her career goal of working as a professional commercial and film actress. The desire to be a "traditional mommy" while her children are young convinced her she could pursue both if she were primarily home-based for now. "I feel I was called to Christian drama when I was in college. I've been trying to do this for the Lord ever since. However, I also feel strongly about being there for my son. In all my reading, I've learned that the first three years are the most pivotal in a child's life, and that I need to be home with my son during this period for his spiritual, emotional, and intellectual growth. That's not a magic number with a cutoff point after three years, but I really think it makes a difference. I know I could be working full-time outside to further my career, but working mainly out of my home is what I need to do right now. I know the Lord will provide in my business when His time is right."

Brian works full-time at an outside job to support his family, but he has a part-time, home-based computer business on the side. He is one of the many home-based moonlighters trying to get a business off the ground. "I wanted to start a business, but wasn't financially prepared to quit my full-time job. Working from my home on the side is a safer way to begin. My wife is at home with our children, but she brings in some income as well by babysitting for other working moms. We would both love for the computer business to take off and someday become our sole source of income, but until it does, I will continue to give it everything I have in the limited time available. It's so satisfying for me to see this business grow and to know that I have control over the amount of time and energy I invest."

Heidi worked full-time as a compensation analyst for a large corporation. When her first child was born she took maternity leave, but went back to work when her baby was four months old. Heidi said she and her husband tried a number of different babysitters, but they kept having problems with their daughter. "At first she wasn't being disciplined, but even when we found a sitter that was disciplining her during the day, she was testing us in the evenings. It just wasn't working out."

Heidi missed her little girl, but she and her husband still needed the additional income. They decided to try something different. "We couldn't keep changing sitters forever. We took a step of faith and changed our priorities. I started my own home business. I was working full-time making quite a bit more than my husband, so quitting work was a major change in our finances, not to mention the start-up costs. We really had to trust God. When we finally made the decision for me to work at home, it was like a load had been lifted. Sometimes it's still a minor challenge to trust God for the money to come in, but we know that it's more important for me to be home with my children."

Nancy just wants to supplement the family income, Gary is a professional who has escaped the nine-to-five routine, Barbara has strong career goals but wants to be home for her children's early years, Brian is moonlighting until his business takes off, and Heidi is a former primary breadwinner now working part-time from home. Five very different people. Five very different reasons for working at home. Five individuals who are doing so very successfully.

Statistics tell us there are millions of women in the workforce today, but this doesn't mean that they all love being there, at least not all the time. Working at home is a dream for many people, and it was my dream as well. I know I was not the only person who often found it difficult to juggle my role as wife, worker, and mother. I wasn't the only one to feel guilty after hearing a sermon at church or reading a book about the role of the Christian family and godly mother. There was so much conflict: the need and desire to be with my children; the empty checking account; the desire to be a helpmate to my husband; and even ambition. Along with millions of others, I have been able to make my dream happen. Perhaps you can too.

What was once a "closet industry" is now a growing force in the business world. With the advent of the information age, working at home is quickly becoming a growing trend. The 1988 National Work-at-Home Study by Link Resources, a New York market research firm, showed that—

- 25 million Americans spend 8 hours or more working at home each week.

- 6 million men and women are working full-time from their homes (up from the 1987 figures of 4.9 million full-timers).

- At least 20 percent of the workforce now works part- or full-time at home (that figure is expected to grow to over 30 percent by the year 2000).[1]

All projections suggest that the number of home-based workers will continue to increase significantly over the next 10 to 25 years.

The U.S. Small Business Administration (SBA) conservatively estimates that 2.2 million Americans are working exclusively from home, with women comprising about two-thirds of that number. (This figure is somewhat low compared to statistics compiled by private research firms and home-business consultants and organizations. However, even the SBA predicts that the number of home-based businesses will double during the 1990's.)[2]

In his 1980 book *The Third Wave*, Alvin Toffler set a scenario for people to work at home connected to their offices via inexpensive computers and other high-tech toys.[3] Many people laughed at his "Utopian" ideas, but today we see that his prediction was right. The main reasons include the popularity and availability of affordable home computers and other business machines, the childcare dilemma, the rising cost in time and money of commuting, the opportunity for lifestyle flexibility, and the shift from the industrial worker to the "information" worker.[4]

There are four main types of home-based workers: the self-employed entrepreneur, telecommuters (those working for other people in some type of white-collar profession), pieceworkers (those in industrial-type work), and independent contractors working for a company without employee rights or benefits.

The average home business owner is between 30 and 35 years old, earns an average of $55,000 a year, and spends $5200 a year on office machines.[5] Those choosing to work at home include homemakers, hobbyists, retirees, people interested in a second income, and the disabled.[6] A research associate for Link estimated that 85 percent of home-workers are white-collar professionals (such as consultants, marketers, or writers), most of whom do some of their work by computer.[7]

Some sources say that women are leading the home-business trend.[8] For women in business, two things are happening: They are quickly gaining ground as entrepreneurs and they are realizing that they can slow down their careers for the sake of their children.

Although there are still more men starting businesses, women are making tremendous inroads into the entrepreneurial world and have been called the fastest-growing segment of entrepreneurship. The cover story of *Nation's Business* of May 1989 was "The Age of the Woman Entrepreneur." It cited impressive statistics for women business owners. "From 1980 to 1986, sole proprietorships owned by women rose from 2.5 million to 4.1 million—a 62.5 percent jump during a period when the number of male-owned businesses increased 33.4 percent. Also during that period, women-owned businesses' receipts nearly doubled, from $36 billion to $71.5 billion. Add the 433,000 sole proprietorships that are jointly owned by husbands and wives and the yet-unknown numbers of women-owned partnerships and corporations, and the figures on women-owned companies would be even higher."[9] Since women-owned businesses have grown from 5 percent in 1972 to 30 percent of the country's sole proprietorships by 1986, some are predicting that by the turn of the century women may own half of the country's small businesses.[10]

While we're looking at women in business, let's consider the so-called "mommy-track." It's the new catchphrase for women juggling kids and careers who do not want to abandon their corporate strides for their toddlers' strides indefinitely. The cover story of *Business Week* on March 20, 1989, detailed how female managers and professionals with young families are leaving the "fast-track" for the "mommy-track." "They are searching for new ways to balance career goals and mothering—a human place to stand, if you will, between Superwoman and June Cleaver. Their employers, worried about losing top performers and attracting talented women in years to come, are beginning to help. They are offering alternative work patterns, from flexible hours to job sharing to telecommuting. In the process, they may be changing the nature of work for men and women."[11] While all of this definitely has redeeming value, aren't we really talking about a new way to have it all—the 1990's approach to assuaging the guilt of chasing corporate "mogulhood" over the career of motherhood?

At first glance it appears that the mommy-track is just the ticket for highly ambitious women: understanding bosses, job sharing, and time off for childbirth and infant-raising without sacrifice in the corporate world. But most of the women profiled in stories like these have one thing in common: They pride themselves in being corporate women over being cookie-baking moms for the long haul. Case in point: "Many women believe they can slow down at work for a few years, get their kids launched, and come back with renewed zest."[12] But children are not rockets needing to be launched; children are gifts from the Lord needing to be nurtured over time. The mommy-track may look like it is the answer to one of the biggest social concerns of our day, but it really only continues to push the view of the fulfilled woman as the woman with the career, except that now she is being offered more than just six weeks of unpaid maternity leave. It is good news that at least big business is actually seeing that children need their moms and that many mothers *want* extended time off for the children while they are small. It is good news that more and more companies are offering creative solutions such as extended leave, flexible scheduling, job sharing, flex time, and telecommuting. These may be promising options for some, especially single working mothers. Just be sure that you are able to see the liberal bias in all the reporting on the subject. We are seeing more working moms, but at least some of them are starting to ask the question "What am I doing? Is this what I really should be doing *at this time* in my life?"

The mommy-track makes the covers of magazines. Mommies who stay home with their children do not. Move over, mommy-trackers, the home-business trend has arrived! Slowing down the career path to make time for the family is a good idea; making time for a home business while raising a family is an even better one.

Government Seal of Approval

In November 1988 the Labor Department lifted a 45-year ban on homework restrictions in some apparel industries, thereby opening the door for many home-based workers doing piecework. The federal government basically said it was convinced that those areas could be made legal again without giving rise to safety or exploitation problems. That ruling affected five apparel industries, now allowing them to hire home-based help to work on gloves, mittens, embroideries, handkerchiefs, and certain jewelry. That could mean opportunities for over 75,000 people to work from home.[13]

The ban originated back in the mid-40's, when the labor department was under pressure from some labor groups and some child-welfare activists to place a ban on certain types of homework. However, homework today is quite a bit different from what it was then. Primarily it used to be an industry function; today it is more often service and information oriented.

Bill Mattox, a senior policy analyst with the Family Research Council, explained what precipitated the lift of that ban: "A lot of businesses were interested in being able to use home-based workers. I think the changing dynamics of the labor force was an important factor, coupled with the fact that you've got a lot of mothers who would like to be home with their children and able to care for them on a full- or almost full-time basis, but who felt some sort of economic pressure to help their families make ends meet. I think this has appealed to many people as a good solution to that particular problem."

Mr. Mattox says that about 20 percent of the labor force is home-based, depending on how you define workers. "There are a lot of home-based workers who are not full-time workers. They are women supplementing their husband's wage and are employed from a few hours a week to 20 or 30 hours, and there are many full-timers as well. It's not exactly 20 percent of the total productivity of the United States that is done at home, but in terms of actual workers it does come out to that."

Telecommuters

Home-business owners are not the only ones opting to work where they live. New technology is encouraging many corporations to offer some employees a chance to work out of their homes as well, thereby creating the telecommuter. Link Resources estimates that some 5 million people work for other companies from home via computer equipment. Some estimates cite 350 U.S. companies offering home-based work to employees, including J.C. Penney, The Travelers Companies, Honeywell, Aetna, AT&T, and IBM.[14] This trend is largely due to the relative affordability of home-office equipment. Personal computers, copiers, and fax machines are commonplace today, and big business is trying to cash in on the office-at-home trend, estimated to be a $5.7 billion market.[15]

There is escalating evidence of the home-business trend as depicted in the media. No longer are stories about home businesses being tucked at the back of magazines or in the "lifestyles" sections of newspapers. We've graduated to the front page. The cover story of the August 1989 issue of *Modern Office Technology* depicts a newly stocked home business. Still-boxed computer equipment is sitting on the patio in front of the "home-office." Articles like this show that there is a growing acceptance by corporate managers, the media, and entrepreneurs that working at home is okay.

Working at home is not only a wonderful opportunity for women, but for men as well. Some men work at home full-time through their own businesses. Some telecommute, but others (as a recent study conducted by *Modern Office Technology* demonstrated) find that the home office allows them to be with their families more when the corporate office expects overtime. Some male-dominated professions lend themselves especially well to partial home-based work. This is a very exciting aspect of the home-based employment trend because it's one way to allow men to become more involved in family life. Bill Mattox, with the Family Research Council, said it well: "Men or women, it may not be possible in every situation to work exclusively at home, but certainly the more home-based work we can provide, the better the opportunities for our families."

Success Stories

It has been said that everyone has at least one "great idea." Those who turn their "great idea" into a successful enterprise are the few hardworking, industrious entrepreneurs who have what it takes to be in business for themselves. A small business doesn't have to be just a "mom-and-pop" type operation.

There would be no such thing as a Hershey Bar if Milton S. Hershey hadn't begun making and selling candy in 1876 from his home in Lancaster, Pennsylvania. If at first you don't succeed, try, try again! Mr. Hershey went bankrupt on the first go-round, but tried again and succeeded in the caramel business. He went on to make the hometown of his factory, Hershey, Pennsylvania, the chocolate capital of the world.

At 40 years of age Colonel Sanders decided to add fried chicken to his gas-station diner. Although he did not begin to franchise until he was 66, his business now includes 7500 stores in 50 countries.[16]

And of course everyone knows about Mrs. Fields. The famous cookie lady began her nationwide cookie franchise business right in her own kitchen. Today you'd be hard pressed to find a mall without a Mrs. Fields Cookies franchise.

For every famous success story there are thousands of other entrepreneurs who are not well-known but are making their home businesses soar. Here are some of the men and women out of the spotlight who decided to embark on this new breed of entrepreneurialism.

Karen White, Richardson, Texas:

I was working in an office when my son got a bad case of chicken pox, and was home for three weeks. I had to work in the office from 6–8 A.M., come home and care for my son, and then go back to work from 6 P.M. to midnight after my husband came home. That was the breaking point. I knew I wanted to be home and available to my son. A couple of weeks later I was asked to be room mother for his school which I couldn't do with an outside job. My quilting teacher then told me about a company that needed help and my home-based appliqué business was born. Through the Lord's intervention and leading, I was able to take the step of faith necessary to quit my job and work out of my home.

Tammy Purcell, Caldwell, Idaho:

In 1984 I gave up a career of nine years as a medical technologist. God convicted me that I was putting the needs of the hospital above the needs of my family. Even though I just worked part-time, the stress still took its toll. Attending numerous arts-and-crafts festivals impressed me with one fact: The majority of spectators would not purchase craft items; they would, however, purchase something *edible*. Four years ago I developed a bean soup mix to sell at a holiday open house. The craft items sold well, but my bean soup mixes *completely sold out* on the first day. Excitedly I phoned my husband. "Bring home more beans!" Since then we've developed six bean soup mixes and five bread mixes. My husband lends his support and expertise on business procedures, bookkeeping, computer applications, etc. Since our specialty foods business is very seasonal, I work full-time from September through December. The wonderful difference, though, is that I'm home and can set my work schedule to mesh with our family activities.

Stella Montgomery, Plattsmouth, Nebraska:

Eight years ago I decided to start a dog grooming shop. As soon as I started, the phone rang off the hook. I had no grooming experience, but had a lot of experience working with animals. I used an all-breed grooming book, bought basic equipment I needed for a couple hundred dollars, and away I went. My first year was the hardest. My income has gone up every year, and I now work 25 hours maximum a week and make $15,000 a year. I have it down to where I can make $9.00 to $15.00 per hour. I work 9:00-3:30 on weekdays so I can help get the kids off to school in the mornings, and be available for them after school. I am truly blessed to be able to stay home and make an income at the same time—and be with my kids!

Sandy Ceto, Du Quoin, Illinois:

I have been a sales representative for Home Interiors and Gifts, Inc., for 3½ years, and can attest to the importance of this type of career for mothers. It allows for Christian growth, personal growth, and career growth without creating sacrifice on the part of our families. There are over 35,000 female sales reps in this company alone, and probably more than 100,000 in the other various party plan companies in the U.S. This enables us to be entrepreneurs as well as involved parents.

Working at home is indeed a trend that will escalate in the years to come. While the way in which we work is new, the idea itself is not. Within one century we have gone from an agricultural society, where families worked together and cottage industries were common, to the industrial age, where business moved to the city. As we enter a new century, we are seeing a surge toward the past. People are rediscovering what our forefathers knew: It's pretty nice to work at home.

2
The Motivation

If the number of people who are working from home today is growing like gangbusters, there must be some pretty good reasons why. The reasons are many and varied, but the underlying theme in all of them is *control*. You, not an employer, are in control of your life.

The Family

Without a doubt, the number one reason I work from home myself and advocate it highly is because it enables me to put my family ahead of any career I might have. George Bush put it well when he said in a 1989 speech, "I believe that family and faith represent the moral compass of the nation, and I'll work to make them strong. For as Benjamin Franklin said, 'If the sparrow cannot fall to the ground without His notice, can a great nation rise without His aid?' " To be a truly great nation we must get back to the crux of strong families and faith. We must quit letting society dictate the family structure.

I personally like the idea of the traditional family where Mom stays home raising her own children, Dad is the main provider, and both parents are dedicated to loving and serving the Lord and teaching their children to do likewise. However, making ends meet in the 1990's is a little rougher economically than it used to be. With over half of all women in the workforce today, the traditional family as we have known it is becoming about as rare as the buffalo: You can still find one if you want to, but they no longer inhabit the earth in the great multitudes that they once did.

Because figures on the numbers of women in the workforce are astronomical, many people claim our country is in a "daycare crisis." A Ph.D. writing in a Texas newspaper said, "There's no doubt that our country suffers under a shortage of adequate childcare services. Our need is staggering. One-third of our homes are headed by a single working parent. Of the remaining two-parent homes, half are headed by parents who both work outside the home. What is available to parents seeking alternative childcare services?"[1] I'll tell you what: home businesses!

Bill Mattox with the Heritage Foundation said, "I think that one of the things that is propelling the homework movement is a recognition that we must be providing as much parent/child interaction as possible. Homework certainly does that better than many other work arrangements."

Many parents earnestly desire a way to bring in additional income while remaining the primary caregiver for their children. Working at home provides more time to enjoy and nurture those little gifts from the Lord. While working at home with preschoolers is indeed a challenge, it is also a privilege: You have the opportunity to be the main molder of character in your child's life, and not just in the evenings and on weekends. It's a nice feeling to share a coffee break with your little one and a worn copy of *Winnie the Pooh*. It's nice to occasionally finish some paperwork with your baby on your lap. You don't have to give up those impressive "power lunches"; now they just include people under four feet tall instead of business associates, and peanut butter and jelly instead of steak.

It probably would have been much easier for me to put the kids in daycare and get a full-time job. While I helped my husband meet the monthly mortgage I could have added to the "working mother" statistics and so-called daycare dilemma. Instead, I found a home business as a way to contribute economically without making me sacrifice the very thing I hold most dear on the earth—my family. Children are little for such a short time. I don't want to miss all the joys of parenting and all the opportunities to make a difference for the Lord in the lives of little people who hang on your every word, desiring to emulate Mom and Dad.

I have great empathy for the single working parent. At one point my husband traveled a great deal and I was in essence a "single mom" Monday through Friday for almost two years. I know how difficult that road is.

One woman in Connecticut shared this story with me:

> I was a single parent for nine years, and during that time God taught me a lot about myself. When my husband first left I thought I would go crazy! He left no money but plenty of bills, and all were at least three months in arrears. At first I worked three jobs outside my home to try to catch up, but I was quickly exasperated and almost never got to see my daughter. I finally put my finances in God's hands and reminded Him that He had promised to meet my needs.
>
> He showed me many ways to bring in money without leaving home, and many ways to have my child with me. They included making and selling crafts, sewing, and performing gospel concerts, skits, and puppet shows. My daughter soon enjoyed working with me.

I also feel for the mother working full-time. I have been there too. I have had to leave my child from 8:30 to 6:00 with another care provider while I went off to work.

I did that on days when my child wasn't sick, but just enough under the weather to make me worry. I did that on days when both of us would rather have stayed home and cuddled on the sofa with books and hot chocolate. I did that on days when my child tearfully cried, "Mommy, please don't go to work today," and those were usually the days when I cried the rest of the way to work.

As difficult as working full-time outside the home was at times, I liked doing what I did once I got to work. I understand why so many women are bent on climbing the corporate ladder. Sometimes it's nice to get a pat on the back for a job well done instead of a pat on the knee asking for more juice. It's nice to feel intellectually stimulated and needed. It's nice to see the results of your efforts in a tangible way. It's nice to be with adults during the day. I understand why many women love working, why it's fun at times, and how it's heart-wrenching at times as well.

I haven't always been at home. I have worked full-time outside the home, part-time outside the home, freelance, and at home for another employer before I began working at home for myself. I experienced the difficulties of each situation, which is why I sing the praises of home businesses. The bottom-line source of conflict in most of those working situations is the need and/or desire for working versus the need to have the kind of home life we want.

Working at home has enabled me to meet the economic needs of my family and has stimulated me intellectually without putting those things above my family life. I am always available to my family first. The world may tell you that this is no way to run a successful business, but look what the world has done with the success of the family. (Besides, there's a lot more in the Bible about succeeding in family life than in business life!) I definitely want a successful business, but not at the expense of things with eternal value.

When I was working in a high-stress, high-pressure job I had a conversation one day with a man who told me something I'll never forget: "Don't sacrifice the permanent on the altar of the immediate." That's what I had been doing: The immediate was my job, and the permanent was my family. That man's name is Tim Kimmel, and his book, *Little House on the Freeway*, is on my recommended-reading list. He made me realize how little by little I was letting external immediacies take precedence over things that had permanent value.

Kristine Staten of Medford, Oregon, runs a family daycare service in her home and explains the importance of putting the family first: "When I worked outside the home, the housework was never caught up, dinner was always late, and there was never enough family time. Now that I'm home, I can do my job during the day and the housework too. Then, when my husband comes home and the daycare kids leave, we can have a nice, relaxed evening together. The very best reward of all, though, is being with my son and seeing him grow and learn. I'm glad I didn't have to miss that."

Time Flexibility

Time flexibility, otherwise known as "you set the schedule," is one of the biggest advantages of working at home. There is no policy manual dictating when your workday will begin and end, and at what time coffee breaks are allowed. If you are ill for a week and the manual allots only three sick days, no problem. You don't have to be employed for a year before you can take vacation days. If little Johnny is the giant carrot in the school play and the curtain goes up at 2:00 in the afternoon, you can be there. If you feel like taking some time off or burning the midnight oil so you can help out during "business hours" at your church's vacation Bible school, it's your decision. Many self-employed home-basers put in more hours each week than those punching someone else's clock, but deciding *if* you want to and *when* you want to is up to you.

Judy Johannesen, who runs a professional calligraphy business from her home in Haymarket, Virginia, describes some of the benefits of her home business. "I love being able to work around school schedules, my Bible study, and volunteer work. I also like the fact that it is part-time."

One home-worker I know gets up at 4:30 each day and puts in at least three hours of work at her business before changing hats to take care of the needs of her family. After the kids are at school and her husband is at work she's back at it until 3:00 in the afternoon. That way she is able to work a full-time schedule with her business, yet be home and available for her family when they need her.

And then there are those (like me) who are allergic to morning. I find my creative juices flowing late at night. That works out great for me because I am able to spend time with my kids in the morning and then often work in the late evening. I don't even have to think about being dressed and alert for the business world at the crack of dawn while I'm still cleaning out the cobwebs in my head. If I'm on a deadline I may work way into the night. That way the next day I won't feel pressured to put in the hours to make that deadline—I can still take the kids to gymnastics or gather the brood and go for a walk!

You're the Boss

When you work at home for yourself, you are the boss. You don't have anyone telling you when to attend staff meetings, make reports, or do paperwork. There are no annual reviews with superiors. There is no corporate protocol (other than what you determine), no time clock, and no procedures manual.

Think about the things that might bug you about working for someone else: the way or frequency in which you are paid, benefits, hours, office policy, the personality of the boss, the philosophy of the company, the ethics of your boss or co-workers. With you as the boss you are in control of all these things and more.

If you have worked for others and thought, "If I were in their shoes, I'd sure do things differently," having a home business is your chance. Many people just have a hard time working for others and would enjoy being the top dog. You may be more productive knowing that you are not laboring for someone else. The fruits of your labor will be enjoyed by you, not an employer.

Angela Kopenan had a home computer business in Carrollton, Texas, before moving overseas and starting her business again there. She started her business for a variety of reasons. "The first is that I hate working for someone else (and I don't make the kind of money that I want to make), but I also want to be more in control of what my family is doing. I want to be there after school and I don't want daycare. I want more control." When you're the boss, that's exactly what you have.

You Decide the Dress Code

While it is just as important to convey a professional image when working from home as it is at the office, you decide what that means. If you want to get dressed up every day, that's great (especially if you deal with clients often), but if you're working all day with no one around but the kids, comfy sweats may be just the right touch.

Many of the home business books tell you to get dressed each day just as if you were going out to the office. I don't know about you, but I'd feel pretty silly sitting at my computer in my suit, hose, and high heels with no one around but me and my children. Besides, think of all the people out there in corporate America who think "Which tie am I going to wear today?" or "All of these hose have runs! I'd better stop at 7-Eleven on the way to work." The home-worker simply isn't faced with that problem.

Increased Productivity

When you have a home business there is no idle chatter around the watercooler unless the kids want to talk with the Sparkletts man when he drops off your new 10-gallon jugs. Think of all the wasted time in an office environment! If you've been there you know what I mean. If not, your imagination could set a pretty good scene. You arrive at your desk in the morning to be greeted by the girl who occupies the desk next to yours. She lost her dog, wrecked her car, took her mother for surgery, and broke up with her boyfriend—all since she saw you at 5:00 last night. And she's not sparing you any details. Then you walk down the hall to turn in a report and bump into another co-worker with whom you needed to talk, but you end up talking for 15 minutes instead of five. You get a cup of coffee in the break room and three employees are titillating each other with the juicy gossip about Susie-So-and-So's latest affair. Yes, offices can be nasty places!

In *Working from Home*, Paul and Sarah Edwards say, "With fewer interruptions and the absence of office politics, people find their productivity goes up considerably. Electronic Services Unlimited's study of telecommuters reports that productivity gains of 40 to 50 percent are realistic."[2]

Telecommuters aren't the only ones to gain productivity. Entrepreneurs enjoy that benefit as well. The *Wall Street Journal* reported the following:

> Numerous entrepreneurs find that their new ventures really do help them escape the strains of corporate life. After 28 years with

an office-equipment company in New York, Harold W. Hobbs started the Paper Warehouse Co., a retailer of paper and party goods in Norwalk, Connecticut. Instead of supervising 500, he found himself supervising four. But, he adds, "I had more worries when I worked for a corporation because there were so many people who could mess things up." Besides, he no longer makes the business trips that used to take 60% to 70% of his time. "We are living an extremely civilized life," says the 54-year-old new entrepreneur. "Now my wife and I even have lunch together."[3]

No Commute

How would you like to have an additional 20 hours a month? Think of all the things you could do with an extra 20 hours each month! Since there will never be a 36-hour day, you're probably out of luck unless you're presently a commuter opting to start working from home. A 30-minute commute is about average for people traveling to their workplace. That's five hours a week round-trip, or 20 or so hours a month, that you can do with as you wish by alleviating the commute! That's a lot of extra time to play with the kids, read a book, go on a family outing, enjoy a hobby, and yes, even work.

Think of the stress that would be alleviated without rush-hour traffic! No traffic jams, no red lights, no crazy drivers. No being late to work because of an accident or construction on the road. Home-business folks certainly aren't holed up in their houses forever, but their auto mobility isn't mandated by the morning and evening drive times, either.

Include the Family in Your Work

With a home business you are free to involve your

family as much or as little as you wish. Many husbands and wives work well together. Many parents incorporate the help of their children in the business, teaching them important values and work ethics while sharing family time.

Keven Knewtson's extended family is involved in their home-based enterprise spanning several generations. "I work with my father and mother in our own business, a coffee service. We deliver coffee to offices and breakrooms in a four-state area. My father started his business in 1969, a year after my grandfather started his coffee service. I have a relationship with my grandparents and parents that wouldn't be possible if I didn't work with them. All these years we have been running things from my father's home, and my grandparents' from theirs."

Donna Gaddy works with her husband in their home business in Channelview, Texas. "My husband and I are fund-raising representatives for three companies now. You are probably familiar with products that schools and Little Leagues sell to raise money for their groups. This is a way that people can make their own schedule and work out of their own home. It's not easy getting a business started and a territory developed, but it is a good way for my husband and me to work together out of our home and make a good living. It has worked well for us."

Diane Austin of Savannah, Tennessee, incorporates her entire family into their home business. "I had always wanted to be an artist, but couldn't afford my dream of college or art school. I took a short course in oil painting and found that it came easily and seemed so natural. It was a God-given talent that lay hidden and dormant. From that point I bought books and spent each day learning, painting as I went. I sold each little piece and put the profit back into supplies until I had all I needed. That was nine years ago. I have been in business for five years, and my husband has been home with me and in full-time business for three years, making wooden items for me to paint. We take our work to arts-and-crafts shows in the surrounding four states. Our two children work in the shop with their father and also help me on certain things. They've learned the skills of working, management, and earning income (not having it handed to them). We've learned a great deal about being in business for ourselves, plus all the values that the Lord has set for us."

Blessings abound when you work at home. There have been many times when I have been at my computer and tiny arms have hugged my leg as my toddler has said, "Hold you, Mommy. Hold you." Some of the best chats with my oldest daughter have taken place as she colored on the floor near my desk while I worked. There are times when the kids will be in the care of someone else while you are working at home, but you and not your boss decide when, where, and for how long. I can't think of a nicer job "perk" than that!

3
Making the Decision

Are you still trying to make the decision to work at home? Let's look at the decision-making process itself. Deciding to start my business wasn't an easy choice to make. Perhaps my two main reasons resemble yours. First, I wanted to use the gifts the Lord had blessed me with, and second, we needed the income.

My desire for a home business started when my first child was three months old. I was at home all day with my wonderful new baby daughter. I loved being a new mom and felt like I was adjusting to motherhood quite well, in spite of the fact that this was rather out of the timetable I had envisioned.

I knew that with the new baby it would be tough for me to get back into my prepregnancy job of television news. My degree was in broadcast communications and I had a passion for the business, something my husband just couldn't relate to. (He asked me, "How many accountants do you know who say they feel 'driven' to account?")

One of my dear Christian high school friends and college roommates was also a "journalism junkie." We made a pact in our sophomore year of high school: "Never get married before 25 and *never* have kids!" Now, lest you think me an unchurched heathen, I was far from it. I just had a drive to get things accomplished careerwise, and I was also influenced by the ever-growing anti-family, pro-career society that was especially promulgated on the college campus.

That roommate broke our pact before we earned our degrees by getting married, and I was next when I had my first child early in my marriage. The whole point of this is that God plants desires and abilities in us and changes hearts for specific purposes.

While I was pregnant I began to feel convicted to stay home with my baby, even though I still wanted to use my gifts for the Lord. I began to pray and read Christian books promoting strong traditional families, motherhood, and being a godly woman. God changed my desire for being the next Dianne Sawyer to that of being a stay-at-home mom. What He didn't take away were some of the abilities, talents, and motivation He had created within me.

I struggled with guilt over having "ambition." I just didn't know what to do with it! I loved my new role as wife and mother, was blessed with a strong Christian husband, and was growing in the Lord. Yet there were days when mild frustration would rear its ugly head. For example, an especially exciting news story would break and I'd think how much fun it would be to cover it; my college friend would call and tell me about her latest reporter stint at "XYZ"-TV; I would read an author bio at the end of an article describing her "blissful" life as a mother and freelance writer.

But I snapped back to reality quickly when I thought of getting back into the grind of a job now that I had this wonderful child sleeping in her cradle. My poor husband tried his best to understand how I could be so dedicated to being home with our new baby and yet experience occasional frustration as well.

Struggling with the desire to use some of the gifts God has given me was just one factor in wanting a home business. The other was on a more mundane level—money. We really wanted to have a traditional one-income family, but it's tough at times to make it on one income in a two-income society!

Getting a full-time job would have seemed like a logical answer. I could have had that "ambition thing" dealt with and have brought in an income alongside my hardworking husband. But when I began to seriously think about it, I got knots in my stomach and tears in my eyes. I really did want to be home!

So what's a mother to do? I had reached the state where I desperately wanted to make money at home, but didn't have the foggiest idea of how to go about it. I had moderate sewing ability and tried making baby quilts. I made a grand total of two! I wanted to write, but didn't really have anything to write about that I thought other people would want to read. I tried several other options and managed to contribute enough to get by financially without getting a full-time job for awhile, but I didn't have a clue about anything even remotely resembling a home business. As I mentioned in the last chapter, I experienced quite a few different working situations in order to meet our financial obligations, but I never quit praying for a way to make money at home. Several years later the Lord answered my prayer.

I'm not saying you must wait eons to see your dream bear fruit. That's just how long it took *me* to get to the place where the Lord was ready to answer my prayer. All the different income-producing options in my life, and all the time at home, served a purpose even though it was difficult to see at that point. I was learning, growing, and developing what some call "hidden art." (More on this when we discuss your calling in just a moment.)

So where do you begin? You want to earn an income from home, but you are unsure where to start? Try starting with this little quiz:

1. Do I feel the Lord's direction to do this?

2. Where do I feel called to excel and what really bugs me?

3. What would I enjoy doing and what are my gifts and talents?

4. Does my spouse agree with my decision?

5. Would my family be supportive?

6. Am I suited for working at home?

7. Is there a market for what I want to do?

8. Have I researched my topic?

Do You Feel the Lord's Direction?

The best place to begin in deciding to start a home business is on your knees.

Before tackling something as important as a home enterprise, spend time with the Lord and be confident that He is leading you in the proper direction and for the right reasons. Deuteronomy 28:2 says that if we are obedient to the Lord He will bless us. Yet how can we be obedient if we do not know His plan for us? How can we know His plan if we are not seeking Him? We must spend time daily in prayer and in God's Word. If you have had trouble in this area of your life, begin now to discipline yourself to spend time with God. At least three-fourths of all small businesses in this country fail within the first five years. With that kind of statistic facing you, be sure you are in the Lord's will and feel His guidance in every step of the decision.

Where Would You Like to Excel?

Many business books tell you to start with your skills and talents, but if you stop there and miss identifying the area where you feel called in life, you could be way out on a broken business limb. Some people say they are driven; others say they are called. Decide if you are in either category.

Sometimes it may take awhile to learn what God has in mind for you. Or perhaps the Lord has been cultivating you for a home business in the things you have been doing up till now. The point is to be alert to what God is doing in your life. Some people know very distinctly that they are called to a task, while others may have an idea but don't know how to implement that idea into a home business.

If you are trying to figure out what you feel led to do, consider the three questions that Mary Pride poses in *All the Way Home*: What do you like to do best? What are you best at? What bothers you the most? Let's start with "What bothers you the most?" Mary says, "The way to find the business that is your calling is to ask, 'What is burning inside me? What do I want to change or improve? What drives me crazy?' You see, the reason you are wondering why everyone else is so selfish/ignorant/ apathetic or whatever about the issue burning in your heart is that God has given this issue to *you*, not to them."[1] Don't complain; get to work! Brainstorm about solutions to the problems that bug you and ask the Lord to give you wisdom.

If you hate the selection of children's clothing in your town, start a line of your own if you have the talent. If you love working with the elderly and hate to see them lonely or in need of a caregiver, start a referral service for live-in or part-time help. If your sole motivation is just to make money, you have probably made a poor business choice. Instead, if you have a passion for the business you have chosen, it will have more meaning to you. If you get all excited about a particular issue, try to make that issue a part of your business.

Mary Pride also says that by doing the humble things in life with zest and unto the Lord, you cultivate skills for your business and you give God an opportunity to open doors for you. This can be called "hidden art," as Edith

Schaeffer describes in her book *The Hidden Art of Home-making*. Mary says, "The point is that while you are trying to become excellent at everything you do, one of your tasks will emerge as your calling."[2]

During the period of time when I began to pray for a home business and the time I actually started one, the Lord had many opportunities to develop hidden art in my life. At one point prior to my home business I was working for a Christian advertising agency. I got to do some writing, but primarily I worked on a computer. I had never touched a computer before that time and I didn't relish the idea of touching one then. I would have told anyone that I did not have the temperament or inclination for such machines. I have to call my husband if the can opener won't work and am basically allergic to anything with an on-switch.

However, the training and experience I got there was the starting point of my home business a short time later. I also began to write as much as I could. I wrote in my journal and volunteered for writing assignments at church and for my employer. The Lord was also teaching me on the home front. I was learning much in the repetitive things of life such as housework, child-rearing, and organizational skills. Even though I didn't know it at the time, He was developing "hidden art" within me and helping me see how I could put my calling into action. Working on a computer in an office was a humbling task for me. Doing the dishes, disciplining the kids when they needed it, and learning how to be organized wasn't (and isn't) always fun either, but the Lord used those disciplines to open a door and answer the desire of my heart.

You see, the Lord can teach us when we least expect it. A friend of mine, Brenda Koinis, was a dedicated full-time mom. Her husband, Steve, discovered that he had an extremely high cholesterol level, so she created an original oat bran muffin recipe for him. She diligently baked dozens of them for him every week, muffin after muffin after muffin. A short time later they felt the Lord leading them into a business with their muffins. If she had grumbled in the small, routine tasks in life (like having to bake several dozen muffins for her husband week in and week out) she probably would not have been open to the Lord's direction for their business. Again, God used a humbling, routine task to open a door for this couple. Hidden art created a business. They didn't start a muffin business because baking was fun; instead, they felt called to a task.

Brenda said, "There was no 'I'm going to start a business. How should we do that?' We had tried that. We had done everything that a person can do to try to start a business, but it was just never right. We talked about at least a hundred business ideas in the past, but none of those ever led anywhere. They simply weren't inspired by the Lord. But this time when we started talking about a business, it was different. This started out with our need and then led to the realization that other people must have the same need. The Lord's leading began with a conversation between my husband and me. It didn't stop there or get put on ice. The next day we were putting action to our plan."

What Are You Good At?

After you have put much prayer and thought into your calling, list all of your interests, hobbies, and talents. Sometimes identifying your calling brings to mind an obvious home business choice. If it doesn't, sit down with paper and pen and write down all the things that you really enjoy doing. If you don't like what you're doing, there is no point in making a business out of it. Then write down all the gifts you feel the Lord has blessed you with. (Don't say you don't have any gifts; everyone has at least one!) Lastly, write down all your talents. Perhaps you feel called to work with children, or do ministry work, or help the elderly, or write, but a business doesn't just spring to mind. Go to the lists you just made. If your calling is working with children and one of your gifts is teaching, you could start a family daycare center or teach kids gymnastics, piano, or anything else that might be on your talent list. If you have a heart for the elderly (your calling), and you like to shop (your interest), and you are good at details and organization (your gift), you might want to start a shopping service for the elderly. Get the picture?

This selection process may be elementary for the person who distinctly knows what the Lord is leading him or her to do. If you are such a person, just count your blessings and skip this chapter! But many other people struggle with exactly what they can do. If you are one of these, don't despair. Go prayerfully before the Lord, then organize your calling, interests, gifts, and talents on paper, and then continue to pray. You'll be surprised at how much clearer you can think when your thoughts are written down.

Don't overlook your hobbies. Many people's pastimes have turned into thriving businesses. One Alabama woman turned her hobby into a full-time enterprise when her pig folk dolls were noticed by a woman who had worked with Xavier Roberts of Cabbage Patch doll fame. That lady suggested that she copyright the design of her dolls. She did so, and soon customers' orders were coming in faster than she could fill them.[3]

If you love to make crafts in your spare time, consider an arts-and-crafts business. If you love woodworking, try your hand at it for profit. If you are a "fixer-upper" and like people and old houses, look into operating a bed-and-breakfast enterprise. The point is to choose something that you would like to do and feel you would be good at.

Does Your Spouse Agree?

If you are married, make sure your spouse is in full agreement with your decision to begin a home business. One home-business owner, Judy Johannesen, wrote me describing how her husband hated the particular product she was selling and discouraged her efforts. When she found something else she could do from home that she would like better, *and* with her husband's full support, everything changed. He even became an integral part of the business. "After a couple of years home with my children I got itchy feet and tried my hand at selling part-time, working around the kids' schedules. It was there that I learned record-keeping and business tax information. However, my husband was not in agreement with me.

"Fortunately, I also took a calligraphy class, and this hobby has developed into a full-fledged business. The best part is that I have the wholehearted support and encouragement of my husband. He's given me lots of marketing ideas, shares a workspace in his shop, and helps in the production. He has also built me a beautiful lettering area, mailroom, and storage space. The Lord has really blessed me with Bob, the kids, and this business, and I pray that He blesses the lives of those my work touches."

Judy's business began to prosper after she adapted her work to God's leading and had the support of her husband. If your "house is divided" you will not experience peace in your marriage or success in your business.

Does Your Family Support You?

While you don't have to have everyone in the house jumping for joy that you are going to make widgets in the garage, it is vital that they support you in your enthusiasm and help share in keeping the domestic train on track. One person cannot run a home business and remain chief cook, bottlewasher, maid, and chauffeur while keeping his or her sanity and health.

It is much easier to withstand the difficulties of a home business if your family is behind you 100 percent. If the kids expect Mom to never miss a beat in seeing to their needs and don't offer encouragement and help in her business endeavors, it's time to do one of three things: Get new kids, throw out the idea of a home business, or involve your children in your work and enlist their help and support. Since the first two ideas aren't so hot, try working with your kids. If they're older and really hate what you're doing, listen to them. They may have valid concerns and could suggest some alternatives to the things about your business that are bothering them. Listen to complaints such as "Mom, we miss you. You seem upset a lot since you began putting 50 hours a week in the business." Complaints like "Mom, I don't like your business because the trash is always overflowing and there aren't any clean glasses" should be dealt with as well. Swiftly lead your children to the trash can as you hand them a garbage bag and direct them to the dishwasher! Sounds like the little darlings could use some frontline involvement in the domestic battle! Working at home is a wonderful opportunity to teach your children about the value of a job well done, a good work ethic, cooperation, family togetherness, and of course business skills. All too many children have no idea what Mom and Dad actually do when they are "at work." Working at home lets them not only see what it is that Mom or Dad does, but allows them to get involved and learn as well. (More tips on involving your children in a later chapter.)

Are You Suited for Working at Home?

Determine if the lifestyle is really for you. If you are a highly structured person who likes a rigid routine, lots of people around, direction from others, and supervision, then working at home may not be for you. If you have just lost 50 pounds and feel the refrigerator would be your constant companion, rethink a home business.

A *Birmingham News* article reported, "Several studies of successful entrepreneurs indicate that they are well-disciplined toward their work, usually are highly competitive, creative, careful about money, have relatives who were entrepreneurs, and often began making money at an early age." The book *In Business for Yourself* lists several characteristics that lead to entrepreneurial success: knowledge of the business you are undertaking; drive, energy, and commitment; persistence; self-confidence; goal-setting; risk-taking; and the use of feedback and outside resources.[4] If one person possessed all of these characteristics in abundance he or she could be called the entrepreneurial model, but ideal business people are the exception rather than the rule. If you abound in one or more categories and you are convinced that you are being led by the Lord to undertake your enterprise, don't let deficiencies in the other categories stifle your dream.

Take inventory of your personality with this "suitability quiz":

- Do you have the organizational abilities and patience to balance a home and a business under one roof, particularly if you have children?

- Are you highly motivated?

- Are you a self-starter?

- Do you set high standards for yourself, or do you perform better when you have outside direction?

- Do you need structure in your life, or do you like a lot of freedom?

- Are you goal-oriented?

- Do you gain pleasure from seeing your goals accomplished, or are you a procrastinator?

- Can you set and meet your own deadlines?

- Do you enjoy being in your home?

- Do you have adequate space for your work?

- Do you need other people around for social interaction?

- Do you need an exciting environment with hustle and bustle to keep you interested?

- Can you adapt easily, or are you a "rigid" person?

Being objective about yourself can be difficult. Carefully consider each question. If you have trouble answering any of the questions, try talking with your spouse, a close friend, or your parents. Ask them how they would answer the questions about you. You may see yourself as a self-starter, but your spouse may see you as a procrastinator. You may not feel like you are patient or well-organized, but perhaps a friend who knows you very well can show you ways that you are.

Working at home will be easier and more productive if you have the right temperament. It helps to be motivated, organized, independent, goal-oriented, and flexible. If you are a chronic procrastinator who is not particularly motivated or enthusiastic and needs a lot of people around, then you will probably experience difficulty and frustration in working at home.

Is There a Market for What You Want to Do?

Make sure there is a market for your product or service. Determine how your product or service is different from what might already be available. How does your product or service help your customers or clients? How is it unique? You need to know, and be able to verbalize, why your product or service is worth paying for. Who would most want to purchase what you have to offer? If you answer "everyone," then you have not done enough market research. Find out as much as you can about the people who need your service or product. You must know who they are and where they are in order to let them know you have something they need. You also need to know how you can reach them. Direct mail? Cold calls? Magazine ads? The way to reach your market varies according to who and where your market is.

Success doesn't depend on being entirely original; it's difficult in today's market to be truly original. But finding your niche is important. For example, if you live in a college town and love doing technical typing with statistics and charts, you may have a niche in the typing market there. Since most people hate that sort of typing, you may have a head start if you see that niche and advertise yourself effectively. Instead of promoting yourself as a general typing service, you might advertise yourself as a *technical* typing service, perhaps even offering pickup and delivery. This even further distinguishes you from the competition.

"Finding your niche" doesn't necessarily mean small potatoes. According to a *Wall Street Journal* article featuring *Family Business*, a new magazine aimed at the family business market, ". . . [this] is a big niche, with at least 1.5 million companies between $1 million and $100 million in annual revenue."[5] Even ventures like *Family Business*, with several million dollars behind it, are banking on a niche in the market.

Big business invests large amounts of start-up capital in market research to actually determine the need for the business. Many small business advisers recommend this as well, but most people beginning home businesses do not have a great deal of money to invest in this area. Market research doesn't have to be done on a large scale by a professional market research firm costing big bucks. Perhaps you could approach it like Edith Flowers Kilgo did, the author of *Money in the Cookie Jar*. She describes how she decided to start selling handmade dolls. Before she began, she did some market research that cost her virtually nothing. She made a model of the doll she wanted to produce (noting the production time and costs) and let her four-year-old daughter run it through the mill (the quality-endurance test). She found several problems and fixed them before ever making a second doll. Next she began to listen to all the comments from people who saw the doll that her daughter carried everywhere. She got a feel for how people felt about the dolls and what they would be willing to pay for them. She gave them as gifts and gained further insight into marketing her craft from the mothers' comments. Through this simplified test of her market she learned about her product's durability, salability, and profit potential before ever beginning production.[6]

Your market research might be as simple as a browse through the yellow pages. If you want to start a secretarial service and there are already 50 of them listed in your small-town phone book (all offering cutthroat competitive prices), maybe you should consider an alternative choice. The old adage is absolutely true: For a successful business, *find a need and fill it*. Just make sure there really is a need.

Have You Researched Your Business Decision?

After you have decided what you want to do (or at least have narrowed it down), research your choice. Learn all you can about home businesses. Spend some time in the library or bookstore and learn all you can about what you are going to do. Read as many books, periodicals, and reference sources as you can about your subject.

When I got serious about my writing, I knew I had a lot to learn. Simply stringing sentences together at the word processor does not produce a published author. I began to research the publishing field. Attending writing seminars and interviewing other authors provided "inside information." What I learned (and am continuing to learn) about the field has helped me a great deal.

As an avid reader of anything written about home businesses, I constantly keep my eyes open for new books on the matter, scan the covers of magazines at the supermarket checkout for articles on the subject, and clip all newspaper articles related to my topic. If you want to start a typing service, check out library books on typing services. If your library doesn't have any listings, check *Books in Print* for titles and get a copy through interlibrary loan, or visit your local bookstore. If you want to sell your handmade crafts or start a home-based import/export business, research all you can about all the aspects of your particular business. Research the product or service itself as well as all the aspects of running a business, marketing, and any other areas in which you need instruction. See the resources section at the back of this book for some research ideas.

Check your local community college or city recreation department for continuing-education courses or non-credit courses related to your field. Many times these classes are available at a nominal fee and cover small-business basics as well as specific instruction in a great number of fields. We do not have to embark on anything blindly; that would be sheer folly in today's information age. There are enough resources at hand to equip and prepare you for your endeavor and to save you from many wrong turns down the road.

Above all, you must be dedicated to your reason for working at home. It has been said that productivity is the by-product of motivation and attitude. You need both the *reasons* for wanting to accomplish your goal and the *attitude* necessary to make the reasons work. If your reason for working at home is six months old and cooing in the crib and you are fiercely dedicated to being the significant caregiver, you have a head start on success because your motivation is so strong. If your *only* reason to work at home is for extra money, then when the going gets tough you may opt to throw in the towel or go the conventional "outside job" route.

4
Home Business Ideas

There's a big difference between people who work *at* home and those who work *from* home. Working *at* home means that you spend almost all your time at home. People who work *from* home use the home as a base of operations, but work outside for some portion of the time. The type of business you choose, *at* home or *from* home, depends on your age, your mobility, whether or not you have children, their ages, if you have supplemental childcare, and how much you want to be away from your home. Some of the ideas listed below are included because the base of such operations could be at home. Some refer to out-of-home businesses which could be adapted to a home business.

An excellent resource for business ideas is *The Be Your-Own-Boss Catalog*, from *Entrepreneur* magazine. It lists 227 business guides that you can purchase or get from your library. Most libraries carry the complete set. They contain the basic information needed to start and operate different businesses. (The series is not *specifically* geared for home businesses, but the information can be adapted for such.) A number next to a business idea shown in the following list indicates a business guide available in the *Entrepreneur* series on that topic. If you cannot find that book at your library, contact *Entrepreneur* magazine. (The address and phone number are listed under Resources at the back of this book.)

The best ideas for starting a home business come from your own personal list of interests, skills, gifts, hobbies, and "things that bug you." This list is just the tip of the iceberg. Ideas for home businesses are all around you. Look in the index of the yellow pages, in advertising that you read in newspapers and magazines, in ads you hear on radio and television, on billboards and company signs in your area, and in conversation with other people. Look for ways to adapt a unique idea or a "traditional job" into a home business. If you are looking for a way to work at home, perhaps this list can trigger a potential business idea for you.

Animals
Pet sitting
Animal breeding
Pet hotel & grooming
  service (X1033)

Computer-Oriented Businesses
Computer consulting
  service (X1221)
Computer repair service
  (X1256)
Desktop publishing (X1288)
Information broker (X1237)
Making money with a
  home computer (X1265)
Research service
Software locator service
  (X1253)
Temporary help service
  (X1221)

Art & Craft Businesses
Alterations
Appliqué
Art broker
Art show promoting (X1021)

Craft businesses (X1304)
Calligraphy
Cartooning
Ceramics
Commercial art
Custom pattern business
Doll making
Drapery making
Flower arranging
Frame making
Glass etchings
Handicrafts co-op gallery
  (X1118)
Jewelry making
Leatherwork
Painting
Pillows
Quilts
Sewing
Soft sculpture
Stained glass
Stenciling
Wall hangings
Woodworking

Employment Services
Employment agency (X1051)

Employment for the elderly
Executive recruiting service
  (X1228)
Resumé writing & career
  counseling (X1260)
Temporary-help service
  (X1189)

Food
Bakery (X1158)
Candy making (X1190)
Catering
Cooking course
Health food/vitamin store
  (X1296)
Homemade cake shop
  (X1094)
Muffin shop (X1295)

Personal Services
Career counseling
Cosmetics (X1135)
Exercise studio
Home organization
Hair salon (X1170)
Image consulting (X1264)
Nail salon (X1274)
Personal shopping service
  (X1310)
Tutoring
Teaching (art, music,
  aerobics...)
Wedding consultant

**Publishing and Writing
Businesses**
Advertising copywriter
Christian consumer
  directory
Classified ads (free)
  newspaper (X1110)

Consumer's helper
Desktop publishing (X1288)
Freelance writing (X1258)
Local cookbook publishing
Newsletter publishing
  (X1067)
Parents' directory
Rental list publishing
  (X1023)
"Who's Who" directory
  publishing (X1026)

**Recreation and
Entertainment Businesses**
Balloon delivery service
  (X1242)
Entertainment agent
Party planning
TV & movie production
  (X1226)
Travel buddies (for single
  or single elderly people)
Vacation planning
Video production company

Services to Business
Accounting
Advertising agency (X1223)
Advertising, specialty
  (X1292)
Bartering club (X1193)
Bookkeeping
Business brokerage (X1317)
Clipping service (X1250)
Collection agency (X1207)
Consulting business (X1151)
Coupon mailer service
  (X1232)
Data processing
Delivery services
Drafting

Envelope stuffing
Graphic design
Information broker
(X1237)
Janitorial service (X1034)
Liquidator—selling
distressed merchandise
(X1098)
Money broker (X1962)
Pest control (X1280)
Plant rental service
(X1049)
Public relations agency
(X1324)
Secretarial/word
processing service
(X1136)
Telephone answering
service (X1148)
Typesetting service
(X1245)
Typing
Window washing service
(X1012)

Services to the Home
Carpet cleaning service
(X1053)
Catering service (X1215)
Closet customizing
(X1291)
Firewood sales
House painting (X1249)
House sitting/in-home
care (X1275)
Ironing
Interior designer (X1314)
Kitchen remodeling
(X1105)
Lawn care service (X1198)

Maid service (X1160)
Pest control (X1280)
Photography
Plant care
Pool cleaning & repair
(X1285)
Shopping service
Window washing service
(X1012)

**Service Businesses,
Miscellaneous**
Budget interior design
Childcare service (X1058)
Event planning service
(X1313)
Gift basket service (X1306)
Limousine service
Nanny agency
Paper collection & recycling
(X1183)
Personalizing items
Printing
Private investigator (X1320)
Reading improvement
service
Scholarship search service
Telephone wake-up service
Travel agency (X1154)
Vinyl-repair service (X1077)

Miscellaneous Businesses
Antique restoration
Auto wholesaling,
customizing, or repair
Bed & breakfast inn (X1278)
Burglar alarm sales/
installation (X1091)
Buying foreclosures (X2327)
Engraving
Fashion design

Flea market & swap meet
   promoting (X1020)
Herb farming (X1282)
How to develop
   multilevel marketing
   sales (X1153)
Import & export (X1092)
Mail-order business
   (X1015)

Public speaking
Real estate company,
   flat fee (X1153)
Real estate investment
   guide (X1284)
Seminar promoting
   (X1071)
Silk flower business
Upholstery

5

Home Business Profiles

The home-based workforce has been called the fastest-growing economic sector in the United States. A recent study showed that it has been increasing at a rate of about 7.5 percent a year, and other sources cite a 46 percent growth in the number of full-time home-based workers since 1985. Some say the number of home-workers has grown by one million people a year for the last five years![1]

With all those people joining the ranks, you would be hard-pressed to find any two home businesses that are exactly alike. That's part of the beauty of having one. What follows are some personal stories of home-based workers across the country who are making a living and loving what they do.

Why are they doing it? How are they doing it? What is the hardest thing they have to contend with? How has the Lord blessed them through their undertaking? They share these things in the following stories.

> One of the most exciting things about our business has been seeing the Lord work in real concrete ways. It's been wonderful to watch the miracles happen. One Wednesday in February, all I had was a notebook of ideas. Just 26 hours later I had 80 labeled packages of muffins and a grocery store buyer taking them

on a guaranteed sale basis! Two days later the store was sold out, and I had my second order.

There were plenty of other miracles, too. Sometimes I would make a string of calls, all appearing to be dead-ends. However, later I would find that the information from those calls was perfect for a situation I hadn't even dreamed of at the time.

Once I went to purchase an electric oven, checkbook in hand. The store had a "Be back at noon" sign on the door, and I couldn't go back at any other time that week. Three days later I found that my baking facility didn't have the right wiring for the oven I was prepared to buy. I see the Lord's hand at work in my business all the time.

> —Brenda Koinis, owner
> Cornerstone Cottage Oat
> Bran Muffins
> Spring, Texas

Working at home is the only way I would work during the early years of my child's life. It is a blessing, but it does have its difficulties. Having time to work in my office, do paperwork, and make phone calls with a preschooler around is my main problem in trying to work in my home. The hardest thing is when I'm working in the evening while my husband watches our son. I shut the door, but it's still difficult to work undisturbed, since my little boy knows I'm in the house. We're still working with that problem. It's getting easier as he gets older.

Sometimes I get discouraged, but I pray about it often. I also try to do something for my business every day. That way I will do 365 things a year for my business instead of trying to accomplish a major thing in one week. It takes the pressure and guilt off.

—Barbara Mayo
Freelance commercial
and film actress
Dallas, Texas

There's nothing better than working at home and being with your children. I worked "outside" for about two years and when my little boy was born I worked in my home doing day-care. Now I work for my dad in his home business and get to take my three-year-old son with me. I don't have to worry about day-care at all. If he's ill, he's right here at home. My Mom gets home at 4:00 P.M., so Grandma gets to watch him in the afternoons. My grandmother lives with my parents, so my son gets to be around his great-grandmother as well. It's a wonderful situation.

—Sherri Forrest
Office manager for her
father's home-based
printing company
Garland, Texas

I have a 14-month-old boy named Nathan and have been a graphic designer/typesetter since age 20. After quitting my full-time job I started freelancing, which still took me away from home more than half the time I worked. Two years later I gave birth to Nathan and had to reorganize my work to be mainly home-based. I have my own drawing board, light table, and art supplies. I only have to leave home to pick up jobs, get type or camera work, and deliver work. In most cases I can take Nathan along with me. I still occasionally fill in at companies when someone is sick or on vacation, and I enjoy the break from home that it brings.

My husband works evenings, so I do most of my errands and fill-in work in the mornings, since we do not want to put our son in daycare. Many of my girlfriends say that I have the ideal situation. However, working at home also has its drawbacks (mainly lack of time spent with my husband). I am enjoying my working schedule and average 6 to 20 hours per week of work, above the job of being a mother.

—Jill Morrison
Graphic designer
San Antonio, Texas

I have been doing daycare for two years now and I'm so grateful for it! Most single moms I know work away from their kids and have to work quite a bit to compensate for receiving a wage which is usually considerably lower than a man might earn. By the grace of God I have a way to provide for us financially while still enjoying the privilege of raising my own children. I earn between $600 and $900 a month on childcare, plus an additional $200 to $325 food reimbursement from the USDA, as I'm a licensed family daycare home. The Lord has really blessed us with this job!

—Jane Agnes Talos
Single mother, home-
schooling parent, and
in-home daycare provider
Talent, Oregon

My husband is a certified public accountant and I have an accounting degree. We both worked for a regional-sized CPA firm for many years before I quit to stay home with our two children. Now our dining room is our home-based office. We have approximately 15 monthly bookkeeping clients for which I take responsibility. We have a personal computer that I use. In addition to these we have around 50 tax clients. I am able to do the majority of the work except during March and April, when we both must work "overtime." My preschooler must go to the sitter occasionally, but often she remains home with me.

We produce a net income of approximately $15,000. If I were to work outside the home I could make double that, but this would be full-time with considerable overtime. We have decided that financially we are better off with me at home if you consider: sitters, clothes, eating out, etc. In addition, I am able to attend school functions, church meetings, and a weekly Bible study. There are many, many advantages and I feel truly blessed to be able to stay home.

The main disadvantage I have found is that people don't realize that I really do work and have responsibilities. I've found I really have to put the word "no" into use more than I like to.

—Kay Roberts
Bookkeeping home-business
owner
Cleveland, Texas

I wanted to share how our family achieved "home orientation." Judie and I have two sons.

The days right after our second son's birth were for me the strongest leading of the Holy Spirit that I have ever experienced. I was being led to this conclusion: We have been blessed with our children to raise and enjoy, to bear witness and live our faith as an example to them, and to spend needed quantity time as well as quality time with them.

After much prayer, meditation, and figuring, we decided that with God's help we can keep the boys at home during their important preschool years by keeping one of the parents home with them.

Although my income was greater, Judie worked only 40 hours per week. Because I worked on commission and Judie had all the insurance and vacation benefits, we decided that I was far better suited to stay home with the boys than she was. I also have a more suitable temperament and am more committed to routine than Judie is.

I'm so thankful we were able to do this. So many families our age couldn't give a thought to one spouse staying home due to debt burdens.

I definitely believe that this is God's will for our family. Some may say it is wrong for the wife to be the major breadwinner in the family, and I can understand that. But I'm still the head of the household and Jesus Christ is still the focus of our lives. This arrangement may not work for everyone, but it is our way (and we believe God's way) of keeping our family "home-oriented."

I've begun a part-time telemarketing business. It allows me to work from my home a few hours per day and puts some money in the bank for us. During this past year we've been able to save more money than in any of the past five years that we've been married.

—Doug Will
Home telemarketer
Sandusky, Ohio

I would really like to tell you about a complete blessing. I didn't start a home business for income; I wanted a playmate for my daughter and began to take in foster children. I soon fell in love with these needy children and over the past five years have led nine of them to the Lord. The state provides financial assistance and total medical care. Although it is not a great amount, it does help and always comes exactly when I need it most. This is actually a greatly needed ministry and I wish more Christian homes would consider doing it. Unfortunately, there are many foster homes which take in children solely for the money. As a result many of these children are abused. Wouldn't it be great to let Christians know that if they would open their homes to these children they would not only receive financial assistance but the spiritual reward of sharing Christ with these children?

—Dianna Stankiewkz
Foster care provider
Moosup, Connecticut

[There are many agencies that place mentally retarded or emotionally disturbed men, women, or children in a foster care setting.]

I stopped working when I was five months pregnant with my son, and didn't go back to work until he was six months old. My husband wanted me to stay home with him, yet we needed the extra income. At first it was only part-time, but then it advanced into a full-time graphic arts position. My son was in a home daycare situation. I hated being away from him so much and felt guilty all the time! You worry whether the daycare provider is good to the kids, since you can never be sure how someone is when you're not around, even though he or she may seem great when you interview him (or her). The only positive thing about it was that it taught my son how to interact with other children.

It's my opinion that it's harmful for a child to be in daycare full-time. Children need their mommies home at least until they start first grade, and I think the mom should be home when they get home from school. I believe it is a mother's duty to take care of her children and home first. God honors that. He's blessed us and provided for our needs. He's made a few dollars stretch a lot farther than we could!

I was only making $4.00 an hour, and $1.25 of it went to daycare. There were clothing and transportation costs, lunches, and then of course taxes. It was almost more expensive for me to work! Then I noticed that my daycare provider made more money a month than I did. She had five children in care at $1.25 per hour, for a total of $6.25 per hour. She didn't have to pay for daycare for her own kids, she could be at home, and she used the USDA food program for registered daycare providers, which reimbursed her for her food costs. That's when I decided to go into daycare. It was perfect because I've always liked kids and I could be at home with my son and still help my husband with our income! Our family is definitely happier for it.

I don't see why more women don't do this, as there is a demand in our country for good daycare for working mothers.

—Kristine Staten
Family daycare provider
Medford, Oregon

6

Setting Up Your Business

Some people have no qualms about whether they are cut out for a home business or whether they have a firm direction from the Lord as to what that business should be. But they may struggle with the next step: "How do I get from *wanting* a home business to *having* one?"

Start-up doesn't have to be a scary thing, contrary to what you may have read. As you delve into setting up your own business, you will be discovering a mass of new information. Even if you think you can remember everything you read and hear, write it down! Keep copious notes on everything you find out, consider, and do in the beginning. You may not think you will need all this information, but down the road it might be just the thing you're looking for. Start keeping organized notes when you begin gathering information, and all throughout your "start-up." Later you will be glad you did. Here is a checklist to help you begin setting up your business.

1. Determine the amount of time you want to devote to the business.

2. Estimate your start-up costs.

3. Determine the amount of money available for start-up costs.

4. From your start-up list, determine your initial priorities.

5. Obtain the proper identifying numbers and licenses, and research federal, state, and local restrictions.

6. Determine your legal form.

7. Choose your name and register it.

8. Open a business account.

9. Have your printing done.

10. Determine your record-keeping system.

11. Establish a business plan.

12. Get your initial equipment and supplies.

13. Decide where in your house you will locate your business.

14. Get organized.

1. *Determine the amount of time you want to devote to the business.* Estimate the time you think it will take to get your business going and to operate it successfully. Make sure you can invest that time to get your business off the ground. If you begin blindly, without any thought as to how much time your endeavor will take (just approaching things as they come along), you are setting yourself up for frustration, if not failure. If you have children, decide at the onset the number of hours each week that you are willing to put your child in substitute care if necessary.

Don't let yourself get in this situation: You embark on what you hope will be a successful business, knowing that it will take a lot of your time but not actually estimating the amount of time you realistically have available. You realize the mess you are in when everything in your home and business needs your attention at the same time and your daily 24 hours is looking hopelessly inadequate. You are overworked and unhappy. You want business success, but not at the expense of your family. The problem: You didn't evaluate your schedule and priorities that affect the amount of hours you have to accomplish "X" in a given day, and so you are going nuts trying to work full-time at everything. (See Chapters 8 to 10 for a more detailed look on how to find the time to manage your home and business.)

2. *Estimate your start-up and monthly costs.* Make a list of what it will take and what it should cost to get your business open. Some advisers say the next step is to double that figure. It may take three times longer than most people think to reach their expected level of revenue in a new business. First-year expenses are usually twice as much as expected.[1] Do not blindly guess what it will cost you to set up; let your fingers do the walking through your phone book and save yourself some time and energy in estimating your costs.

What are some of the things you need? Consider equipment and/or supplies to do what you do, office furniture, a telephone listing or separate line, office supplies, inventory (if product-related), letterhead, envelopes, business cards, licenses and fees, printed business checks, legal and professional fees, and initial advertising. Check around the house before you purchase anything; use what you already have. You will usually find that many items on your list, from paper clips and notepaper to an office chair, can be confiscated from somewhere in your house.

Estimate your monthly expenses as well. You'll be surprised how fast your second month in business rolls around requiring financial support, often before your profit has appeared. Some items require capital only in the start-up phase (such as a telephone business line or office furniture). You also need to know how much money it will take to keep you in business three weeks after you open your doors, four weeks after that, etc. These items include your telephone bill, supplies (particularly if you are product-oriented), advertising, and anything else that you will need on a monthly basis in order to operate.

3. *Determine the amount of money available for start-up costs.* After you know how much money it will take to get started, decide where the money will come from: personal savings, family contributions, personal bank loans, small business loans, investors, etc. Will you need a lot of start-up capital, or a little? Will you need a loan? Can you use part of your savings? Some businesses can begin on a shoestring and require little more than sweat of the brow to get going. (Great way to start!) Others take considerable financial investments to begin. If yours is one of the latter type, your best bet would be to wait until you have the amount of start-up capital you need on your own, or else to reevaluate your business choice.

The best way to begin a home business (especially for people with little or inadequate business training) is to begin small. Start out small and manageable, and aspire to grow. Don't aspire to begin big and then end up with nothing but giant debts and a broken business.

Barbara Brabec in *Homemade Money* says, "Few individuals are able to get a bank loan at the start of their home business, either because they lack start-up capital or the kind of collateral the bank requires, or they're simply reluctant to pledge to the bank what collateral they do have, usually savings accounts, equity in a home, or cash surrender value of an insurance policy. In the end, many people decide that it's easier to borrow from their own savings account, or perhaps a relative. Others simply figure out how to raise their own venture capital through a variety of entrepreneurial activities."

The Small Business Administration (SBA) offers many financing programs, but this organization rarely makes a direct loan to an individual or company. It primarily guarantees business loans made by local banks and other lenders to small-business clients. The agency guarantees up to 90 percent of the value of the loan balance. The loan guarantees do not exceed $750,000, and they average about $175,000. The average maturity is about eight years. The SBA says the main reason loan requests are turned down is lack of experience of the small-business client.

If you feel you need a loan to get started, visit your local bank with a well-written business plan. (More details on business plans later in the chapter.) This will greatly enhance your chances. Submit this to your bank. If you are turned down, ask for an SBA loan guarantee. The bank, if interested, will then contact the SBA directly. Do not rush into any financial decisions. If you can start your business without a loan, you will be much better off.

Make sure you weigh the costs before you start. Statistics show that the main reason for small business failure is lack of sufficient capital. Yet if your capital is limited (isn't everyone's?), don't let that stop you; just be realistic in the financial planning of your endeavor by starting small.

4. *Determine your initial priorities.* From your start-up list, decide what is absolutely essential to get your business going. Don't buy anything that is not necessary in the beginning. At first glance you may feel everything on your list is vital, but after looking at the bottom-line figure of what it will cost you to purchase everything on that list at once, you will probably find a way to prioritize those items. For example, if your business is computer-based and you need specific equipment to operate, figure out exactly what you will be doing the first month.

You may find that you can get by without the hard drive for a month and can purchase the modem in your third month of operation, when you will really need it more. You may have to bite the bullet by not having all the equipment you need in the beginning in exchange for a more comfortable cash-flow position, which is vital to your start-up survival. Be thrifty in what you *do* have to buy. How many widgets will you have to sell, or how long will you have to work, to pay for your purchase?

For example, when I began my company I started out with one Macintosh computer. It was almost the bottom of the line in quality, but it got the job done. Later I upgraded the memory in that machine and even later sold that computer and bought a more powerful one. I gradually added more equipment as I could afford it, procuring some of it through bartering and client financing. I certainly didn't have everything I needed in the beginning, but neither did I have a wealth of start-up capital. I suffered through endless disk-swapping until I could really afford a hard disk. I used a friend's laser printer until I could get my own. It took awhile to get all the equipment that I have now, but financially it was the only way possible without racking up tens of thousands of dollars of debt before I opened my doors for business. Had I tried to purchase everything on my start-up list in the beginning, I probably would never have gone into business at all.

If you want an answering service, but have to pare down your start-up list, consider using an answering machine that you already own, or else borrow one for a short while from a relative or friend if you can't afford it on day one. I wanted an answering service for my business to enhance my business image and to ensure that I would get all my messages and that my clients (most of whom were business professionals) could talk to a human being. Since I couldn't afford this service in the beginning, I used an old answering machine that had been in the family practically since the things hit the market. It gave me a few headaches, but it saved me money and got the job done until I was able to get an answering service.

If your company produces something tangible to sell, you can probably think of a great deal of things you need to create your product, speed up production, and make your work easier. Just be alert to the things on that list that are necessary for you to open your doors and the things that can wait. Many things may seem vital in the beginning, but careful evaluation, prioritization, and a little creativity will reveal what is really essential for start-up and what can wait a month, three months, or a year.

5. *Obtain the proper identifying numbers and licenses, and research federal, state, and local restrictions.* Check your local, county, and state agencies for all fees and licenses that you must legally obtain in order to set up shop. Check with the Department of Commerce in your state. This agency may be able to help you locate other specific agencies that you need to contact for your business. A "Permit to Do Business" is often required. Also check zoning restrictions for your business. Both of these can usually be done by contacting the city planning or zoning department or your home-owners association. One of the most-asked questions about home businesses is "But are they legal?" The answer is probably yes, but check with the city planning department in your area. If you are handling food, your business is probably regulated by the county health department, and regulations are usually more prohibitive. Zoning laws are set by each municipality. A good rule of thumb is that if you do not have an excessive number of clients coming to your door, the UPS or Federal Express man doesn't make daily stops at your home, and you don't have the street blocked or use loud machinery, you are probably okay. However, don't leave anything to chance. Find out if your particular

home business is legal in your area *before* you start it. For example, one man employed several people in his home business. His neighbors complained to local officials, who came knocking at his door.

"Do you have a business in your home?"

"Yes."

"Do you employ nonfamily members in your business?"

"Yes."

"That is against city regulations. You have 30 days to rectify the situation."

Rectifying that situation meant restructuring his business. He had a strong enough desire to keep out of the nine-to-five environment that he found office space for the employees while he himself remained at home. By the way, that situation cost him over $1500 to correct!

I live in a typical suburb of a large metropolitan area. I called City Hall, asked for the planning and zoning department, and asked specifically about restrictions in our community for home businesses. Their answer is probably typical of many areas. Home occupations are not licensed by my city. If I had an office site I would then require a certificate of occupancy by the building inspection department. To stay within my zoning restrictions I must have no outside signs, no employed persons other than the occupants of my home, no outside storage or machinery, no excessive traffic due to the business that might block the street, and most importantly, no complaints. I'm not saying these requirements are the same for your area, but they may be very similar.

If you inquire about obtaining the proper license and are told flatly that home businesses are prohibited, ask another clerk or go above his or her head. Inquire about a zoning variance, or a legal way around the city law. The Entrepreneur Association tells a story about someone who applied for a license to conduct a research business from his home, but was abruptly told by a cranky city employee that all home businesses were illegal. He did some checking and was able to obtain a zoning variance enabling him to operate his business legally.[2] If this kind of prohibition happens to you, find out what kind of variance or conditional-use permit you can apply for, and then make an effort to find someone in the bureaucracy who will help you with the additional paperwork required.

If you are operating outside of a city or town's jurisdiction, then contact your county government. Certain states also regulate various occupations and professions, requiring either a license or an occupational permit. Your state can tell you which occupations require state approval. (Some include: real-estate brokers, insurance agents, plumbers, barbers, health-care professionals.) Other businesses require licensing by the Federal Trade Commission. They do not usually relate to home businesses, but contact the FTC if you feel your business may apply. Federally licensed businesses include radio and television stations, investment advisory services, etc.[3]

If you are a sole proprietor without employees, you may use your social security number as your business number on official forms. Or you can contact the IRS and obtain an application for an Employer Identification Number (EIN). You need this if you have employees or are set up as a partnership or corporation. (Contact your local IRS office for form SS-4.) Call your local tax agency to see if your product or service is taxable. This agency will send you the proper tax forms and a tax ID number that you provide when you purchase items for resale.

6. *Determine your legal form.* Decide whether you will operate your business as a sole proprietor, partnership, or corporation.

Sole Proprietorship

The sole proprietorship is the most common form of

home-business ownership. *Starting and Managing a Small Business of Your Own*, by Wendell O. Metcalf, lists some pros and cons for sole proprietorship.

Some of the advantages:

1. Low start-up costs.

2. Greatest freedom from regulation.

3. Owner is in direct control.

4. Minimal working capital requirements.

5. Tax advantage to small owner.

6. All profits go to the owner.

Some disadvantages:

1. Unlimited liability (if the business goes under, you are personally liable).

2. Difficulty raising capital.

This business form is the easiest and least costly way to begin. The only legal papers required are a business license and a fictitious-name filing with the county clerk. No separate tax returns are required, and you can combine your personal money with your company's money. However, in a sole proprietorship, business creditors can go after you personally. If your business goes bankrupt you must also declare personal bankruptcy, or else pay off all the debts of the company from your personal funds. Your personal credit can be affected for years if your business goes bankrupt.

Partnership

A partnership is a legal form of operation in which two or more people basically operate together as sole proprietors. Each partner has equal authority in business contracts, unless spelled out differently by an attorney. One advantage of a partnership is that it gives each partner freedom from the business at times. If you and your partner have brought equal and appropriate skills and abilities to the business, having a partner can free you to take time off for vacations and provide assistance in making business decisions.

However, one of the biggest problems with this type of operation is that *each partner is fully liable for the other partner's actions*. *Legal Aspects of Small Business*, by the American Entrepreneurs' Association, puts it like this: "In any legal or creditor action, each partner will be sued personally, with property, bank accounts, etc., being attached. If one partner skips town, the others are left holding the bag. Also, when an individual contributes assets to a partnership he retains no claim to those specific properties, but merely acquires an equity in all assets of the firm."[4]

Choosing the right partner is almost as difficult as choosing the right mate. He or she is with you for the long haul. You both have a lot invested in the relationship. You usually don't know nearly as much as you thought you did about the person when you entered the relationship, and often the worst in both people appears after you are "hitched." Even if you have known a person for a long time, don't leave anything to chance. Before you form a partnership, discuss with your prospective partner everything you can think of that might affect your business. Then have a lawyer assist you in drawing up legal papers. That way you are both covered if your partner decides to leave the business, turns out to not work as hard as you, or changes his vision for the business. It is often difficult to remain friends with your partner if the business doesn't go as well as expected, unless you have discussed all possible outcomes of your business at the onset of your partnership.

Corporation

A corporation is more complicated than the other legal forms of business. It is a legal entity apart from you. It is responsible for financial obligations, not you personally, since you are technically an employee of a corporation—even if you own all or the majority of the stock. Here are some of the pros and cons of a corporation:

Advantages

1. Limited liability. (If the business fails, your personal assets cannot be touched. The corporation protects your personal assets.)

2. Banks lend money more easily to corporations.

3. Profits can be delayed.

4. Capital can be loaned to you personally.

Disadvantages

1. Possible double taxation.

2. Higher cost than the other types of business forms.

Subchapter S Corporation

If you set your company up as a Subchapter S corporation you take care of the double-taxation issue. "Subchapter S allows profits or losses to travel directly through the corporation to you and your other shareholders. If you earn other income during the first year and the corporation has a loss, you can deduct against the other income, possibly wiping out your tax liability completely. Subchapter S corporations are corporations that elect not to be taxed as corporations; instead, the shareholders of a Subchapter S corporation include in their individual gross incomes their proportionate shares of the corporate profits and losses."[5]

You do not always need the expense of a lawyer to set up your business as a Subchapter S corporation, although many business books will tell you otherwise. Legal fees can range from $350 to $2000. The forms are often easier to fill out than some credit applications, and you can easily file them yourself. The name you are using is checked by the Secretary of State's office (usually without an additional fee), and this office will tell you if someone is already using that name or a name closely linked to it. *Entrepreneur* has do-it-yourself incorporation kits for all 50 states. These include simple but complete instructions, plus completed samples showing exactly how to fill out the forms and where and how to apply. The kit is about $45. See the Resources section for the mailing address.

7. *Choose your name and register it.* The selection of your business name is an easy choice for some people and a hard one for others. For many it's simply their own name that they lend to their business. Others want a catchy, unique name. The most important thing in naming your company is to choose a name that easily describes what it is you do. Joan's Typesetting Service more clearly defines what it is that Joan does than J.J. Inc. While J.J. Inc. may sound more professional, it doesn't tell you if Joan is an attorney, financial adviser, or hoozyhiemer manufacturer. Joan's Typesetting Service may sound boring, but it gets the point across. You may think of something catchier and more professional than Joan's Typesetting Service, but remember to be descriptive in your name, not just unique.

If your business name is not your own, file a fictitious name certificate with the county. The fee is nominal (usually $10 to $100) and the county will inform you if someone else is already using the name you have chosen. The easiest way to determine the proper procedure for your area is to call your bank and ask what it requires in this regard for you to open up a business account. The bank people can then tell you where to go to take care of this requirement. If you incorporate, file your corporate name with your Secretary of State (who will also do a name search).

8. *Open a business account.* Open a separate business bank account. It is vital that you do this in order to keep tabs of your business expenses and for accurate record-keeping and tax purposes. If you were ever audited, it would be difficult to sort through things without a separate account. The cost is minimal, and all you need is either your fictitious name certificate, tax ID number, or business permit. It is simple to do, costs very little, makes record-keeping and tax time simpler, and looks more professional than writing personal checks for business expenses.

9. *Have your printing done.* One thing you will need is a logo. It may be as simple as your company name in a particular typestyle, or more elaborate, with graphics and artwork. Your logo is important because it is the common identifying element that ties all your printed items together; therefore it should reflect the image or tone of your company. Your logo should also help clarify what it is that your company does. If your business is targeted toward professionals or the financial industry, your logo should be straightforward, businesslike, and professional. If your business is crafts-oriented, let your creativity show in your logo design. What works for one type of business will be totally wrong for another.

Think of the image you want to create. Is your company serious? Lighthearted? Imaginative? Creative? Describe your image to yourself, and then reflect it in your logo, typestyle, paper stock, and color choice. Failure to match your business image with your printed output is a costly mistake to make. For example, a computer book-keeping service probably would not want to have pink hearts on mauve paper for its business card, but that motif could be very appropriate for a children's party catering service.

Your logo will be used at least on your business cards, letterhead, and envelopes, but can be used even more extensively than this. You can have it printed on your invoices and other forms or paperwork that your clients see. And of course if you do any advertising, your logo should be prominent. It is the unifying factor, the physical focal point, of the image you want your company to project. It establishes product or company identification among your clients or customers. It also creates a professional image. Many people will pass a first-impression judgment on your business and your professionalism based on the printed materials you give them. If you hand them a poorly done business card or send out a mailing with mix-and-match papers and plain number 10 envelopes that you can get in the grocery store, you are sending out a message that says, "I'm not serious enough about my business to invest in my printing," or, "I don't pay much attention to detail," or, "I'm really not very professional; I'm just a home business." All these signals are to be avoided like the plague. You do not have to be a graphics-arts major to create excellent-looking printing. Never put off having your printing done just to save money, because in the long run you will lose money by approaching your business venture amateurishly.

Your local printer can help you with paper selections. If you find a particular paper that you like after looking at his samples, ask if there is anything comparable from another manufacturer that might be less expensive. You can often save money this way. Two paper companies may have a very similar type of paper, but one may cost more because it is harder to order, the supplier is out of town, that company's warehouse just had a fire, etc. Or the other paper may cost less because your printer bulk-ordered that paper last month and has an overrun sitting in the warehouse that he could let you have at a discount. However, don't assume that because you say you like a certain paper your printer will know you mean you'd be happy with anything like that. They are used to working from precise specifications; their job demands it. A 20-pound linen paper from one company may be very different from a 20-pound linen from another manufacturer.

When you select your paper consider the color, weight, and texture. All can add to your image when you choose the right combination. For example, if you deal in textiles (clothing, weaving, etc.), a heavily textured paper might be perfect. If you sell brass or glass products, you might want a glossy stock. The paper you choose adds to your image. When you select the color of ink you will use, consider the color of your paper. Often you may like the color of ink you have chosen from the sample book, but when it is printed on a particular color of paper you may get something a bit different than you expected.

After you have chosen your logo, paper stock, and colors for your letterhead, business cards, and envelopes, select a printer that specializes in this type of printing. Don't go to the largest printing house in your town that does mostly four-color process jobs in large runs if you just need a simple printing of black ink on 20-pound bond. By the same token, you might not want a small "quick printer" if you have a complicated three-color logo with artwork and embossing. Do some telephone shopping and try to match your printing job with the right printer to get the best job possible at the best price. It may seem like all printers are the same, but they definitely are not. Another money-saving tip: If you can estimate the amount of letterhead, etc., that you think you will use in one year, your cost per piece for your printing will be much lower than if you were to have to reprint again later.

10. *Determine your record-keeping system.* Keeping accurate records is vital to the success of your business. Don't leave anything to chance. The more detailed your bookkeeping, the better. Keeping track of your business on paper routinely means that you will make more money because you won't miss out on opportunities.

Hiring an accountant is an investment in your business. He or she can help you set up your books, alert you to all the tax benefits to which you are entitled, and keep you up-to-date in paying your taxes. (See Chapter 8 for details on keeping records and setting up a system.)

11. *Establish a business plan.* If you want to achieve your goals, begin by writing them down. For your home business, write your business plan. This is simply a written clarification of your business. A good business plan will clarify your goals and give you a plan of action to achieve those goals. Include:

- A description of your business
- Your goals for future growth
- Start-up costs
- Finances: monthly expenses, monthly sales predictions, your income goal, sales predictions over a given period of time, a balance sheet (what you owe, what you have, and your investment in the company)
- Market research: your competition, your target market, your plan to reach that market (advertising and/or promotions)

- Production: how your work will be accomplished
- Management information: a bio of who's running the company.

The SBA recommends the following information in your business plan if you are going to apply for a loan: the purpose of the loan, the amount of the loan, how you plan to pay it back, a description of the business, a financial profile of the owners and managers, a market description, and a list of available collateral.

A business plan is critical if you plan on getting a bank loan, but even if that is not your objective, take the time to write down your plan. You will know more clearly what your company is all about, how to explain that to other people, where you are headed, and how to get there.

One tax manager described it this way: "The first thing you need to do in starting a business is to sit down and develop your business profile in terms of who your customers are going to be, how you're going to market your services, and where your business is going to be in the next three years as you see it. Without those goals you really don't have anything to go after."[6]

12. *Get your initial equipment and supplies.* After looking at your start-up priorities and the amount of money you have, purchase, borrow, or otherwise obtain the necessary items you need to start your business. Be careful about what you buy. What you think you may need in the beginning may not be necessary later on. Purchase your office equipment on a gradual basis as you discover through working just what your actual needs are. Don't rush out and buy office furniture, a computer, telephone, copier, and fax machine before you are sure you need all that equipment.

Before sinking a ton of money into expensive equipment, check out all your options. Look at your list, then look around your house. Chances are that you can cross off quite a few items that way. In any case, a direct purchase of equipment may not always be the best bet. Comparison-shop carefully before you buy anything, especially the high-dollar items. Certain kinds of equipment or office items (such as furniture) can meet your needs and save you money if you buy them previously owned. However, you should be extremely careful if you purchase electronic equipment used. It is best to buy this type of equipment new, with a warranty and a service agreement.

If you do not have the money you need to get started, renting equipment might be an option if you foresee that you can generate some cash fairly early, then turn around and invest in your own equipment. Suppose you want to start a typing service, but don't have a typewriter or enough cash today to buy the model you really need. If you have some prospective clients and know that you can make some money immediately, then you might want to rent a good typewriter until you have generated enough cash to purchase the machine of your dreams.

Renting equipment also comes in handy when your own equipment breaks down and you have a job to complete. I was once working on a big typesetting job when my hard disk crashed. A computer system that is kaput means unhappy clients. I couldn't get it repaired in time to finish the job on time, so I found a company that rented the equipment, and I was able to meet my deadline. I still made a profit, even after paying the exorbitant daily rental rate. I didn't have to jeopardize my relationship with my client or risk losing the account by being unable to finish the job.

If you are looking at office furniture, used (or "pre-owned," if you prefer) is often the way to go. Check out your home first. Do you have a spare desk in the garage or guest room that you can use? I confiscated my husband's desk until I had enough money in the business account to buy my own, and I also opted for one of our kitchen chairs, since it was free. I bought inexpensive plastic shelving to hold my supplies (since they would be stored out of sight) and I borrowed the corner of another piece of furniture to hold my laser printer instead of buying the nice wooden printer stand that I really wanted. I may have wanted pretty new things to deck out my pretty new home office, but I chose the most economical things instead. My family and I liked the office just fine as it was, and we were the only ones who needed impressing. The smaller the cash outlay at the beginning, the better.

If you don't have much around your house that you can use, check your local paper, the "free" classified papers, and garage sales for quality office items such as furniture, filing cabinets, and typewriters.

When it comes to purchasing supplies, remember that you save money when you buy in bulk. (But try to accurately estimate how much of a certain item you can actually use, so that you're not stuck with 3000 red pens just because they were half-price.) The best places to buy office supplies are generally the wholesale and warehouse stores.

13. *Decide where in your house you will locate your business.* First it was the laundry room. Then it was the dining room. Then it was that corner in the bedroom. They all sufficed as my home office at one time or another. The ideal situation for a home office is your own separate room dedicated to nothing besides your business. This keeps business physically (and hopefully mentally) separated from the other areas of your life. One man I know had his new home built with 1000 square feet reserved just for his home business, complete with separate entrance and atrium. Other people

convert their garages or basements into offices. And many people just happen to have a large spare room that would be perfect for their office. The vast majority of people with home offices make do with what they have. If all you have is a small corner of a room, make sure this corner is devoted strictly to your business.

When you are deciding where to put your home office, keep in mind what your special needs are.

- Do you have the type of business that demands absolute quiet and concentration? Make sure your office has a door that can be shut.

- Does your office have a telephone jack?

- Are there enough electrical outlets, and are they in the places you need them?

- Will there be adequate space for all your equipment and supplies? Remember, your space needs always grow as your business does, so make sure you leave a little physical growth room as well.

- Will the space you have chosen work if clients must visit your work area? If you deal with businessmen in your service business and they have to meet with you in your work area, your bedroom would not be a good idea. But if they only need to drop off and pick up items, never seeing your workspace, a corner of your bedroom would be fine.

- Do you need an open work environment? If you hate being shut up or need to be able to watch your children while you work, try an open area of your home like the dining room. Many people I know have converted their dining rooms into offices that rival a corporate suite.

When outfitting your office, consider ergonomics—the study of human engineering. (Yes, there really is such a field.) That's a fancy term for designing equipment and workspaces to be both functional and comfortable. "Until recently, little attention was paid to such concerns. But as computer use accelerated, workers spending long hours at terminals began to show signs of physical strain that had never before been associated with desk work. Complaints of backaches, headaches, neck and shoulder tension, eye strain, and general irritability led to the emergence of the ergonomics design field."[7]

Such experts recommend the following:

- Writing and paperwork: Work surface should be 28½ inches from the floor.

- Typing or computer work: Work surface should be 24-27 inches from the floor.

- Computer monitor and copyholder should be 16-28 inches from the face.

During this start-up phase, determine what your ideal working environment would be like, the special needs you may have in working at home, and what space you have available; then go from there.

14. *Get organized.* Before you actually "hang out your shingle," make sure your home is in order. Get rid of the clutter, clean out the closets or other areas of your home that need your attention, and know where all of your important papers are. In a nutshell, get your act together if you haven't done so before. Organize your home so that you can find things when you need them without having to tear the house apart in a mad search. Some may say this is no time to do your spring cleaning or household organizing, but I say "au contraire!" When

you embark on something with as much stress potential as starting a home business, it will help to have the other areas of your life as neat and orderly as possible. If you have just spent the day doing "start-up stuff," you don't want to find out at five o'clock that you have five minutes to locate and organize all your insurance papers scattered in three rooms of your house for the meeting that your husband scheduled with a new agent.

Get organized about your daily schedule as well. Buy an organizer or appointment book and write down your appointments, phone calls, and "to-do" list. I live by mine. Just leaving things to memory can leave you frazzled. Being organized in your home and business affairs will make you feel better about yourself and will lead to a more peaceful, productive business and home life.

Starting up your business does not have to be a complicated, drawn-out, scary thing. Seek as many resources as you can for help and advice. Look at some of the options available in the Resources section of this book. A *Wall Street Journal* article on the start-up strain for a new entrepreneur reported that tapping outsiders for advice can reduce start-up panic, often at no cost. " 'If you can network and identify business owners who are established or retired, you can create a group you can go to for advice.' Organized programs arrange for retired executives to provide small businesses with volunteer consulting help. Even before starting the enterprise the entrepreneur can talk to others who have gone through the start-up experience."[8]

Visit your library, talk with friends who have done it, and get all the advice and assistance you can. Seek counsel from both God and other people. The Bible encourages wise counsel: "Where there is no guidance the people fall, but in abundance of counselors there is victory" (Proverbs 11:14). "Through presumption comes nothing but strife, but with those who receive counsel is wisdom" (Proverbs 13:10).

Above all, continue to ask the Lord to lead you as you lay the groundwork for a business that can bless you and glorify Him. "This also comes from the Lord of hosts, who has made His counsel wonderful and His wisdom great" (Isaiah 28:29).

7

Bringing the Workplace into Your Home

———

Living and working in the same location can be both a blessing and a curse. While the blessings are numerous, there is great potential for mass chaos. Imagine what it would be like if a Fortune 500 company president decided to start sleeping at the office to get more accomplished. He's a man with an important job and he doesn't want to spend wasted time commuting. He brings in his sleeping bag, toiletries, and some personal articles. Gradually more and more of his belongings make their way in. He misses his family so they begin to visit him all the time. By now his office is strewn with his personal belongings, looking very unprofessional, and his work papers are sharing space with his electric skillet and toothbrush. The family and the dog are now permanently residing at his office as well. This man with the important job is now up to his neck in alligators. Chaos reigns, and he's getting little done. His office doesn't resemble his office anymore because *home has invaded work!*

Work can overtake your home as well. Your tranquil domicile opens up its doors to a business endeavor. The home business takes off, and now your orderly belongings and lovely decor are cohabitating with a sleeping giant—your business. You are a woman with an important job, that of being a homemaker, wife, mother, and now businesswoman. But "the business" has invaded your domestic retreat. The phone rings off the wall. A steady stream of people pop in continually and at a moment's notice. Your work papers are keeping the dining room table buried. Your laundry is in a big heap because, while your work paraphernalia is abundant, your time is not. You can't get anything done. Your house doesn't resemble your house anymore because *work has invaded your home!*

This second scene isn't pure fiction, because I've been there. Other home-workers have also experienced that same feeling of home/work chaos. Yet it doesn't have to be like that. With proper planning and a commitment to do all things as unto the Lord, you can live in entrepreneurial domestic tranquility.

How? What are the main problems in this area, and how can you avoid them? Let's look.

Keeping Home Life from Invading Work

Let's start with the problem of running a successful business in the midst of a home, its paraphernalia, and its occupants (which in my case includes a husband, two preschoolers, an infant, and a dog). You want to be professional. You want to get as much done in as little time as possible. But there are some problems that our office-residing business counterparts do not have to tackle.

Problem number 1: You succumb to the "I can't get it all done" syndrome.

If you think for a millisecond that you can run your home efficiently and be a business mogul and supermom without delegating some of your tasks, you'd better think again. The best business managers are those who delegate things that do not need their direct involvement. As a home-business owner you can delegate jobs in your business, jobs in your home, or both, depending on the amount of your work and your degree of help. You may need help with the housework, help with the children, help with your business, or any combination thereof. Recognize when you do need help, and then take action to get it. Attempts at being a supermom don't do you, your family, or your business any good. For specifics on this, see Chapter 10 on managing your home.

Problem number 2: You can't mentally divorce yourself from your home surroundings, thereby making it difficult to get started or to concentrate on your work.

People with "traditional" jobs who drive to their place of business don't have to look at a mess all day long if they leave their homes in a state of chaos. The home-business person cannot afford to do this; he or she is stuck with looking at and working in the mess. This is extremely distracting. While some people are very good at blocking out the unsightly array of their home, I am not. If the beds aren't made, there are dirty dishes in the sink, and my den looks like Toys-R-Us, I find it extremely difficult to settle in for a productive morning's work. I may start working, but pretty soon I let a phone call interruption become an excuse for a quick break to make the bed. If I have a particularly busy afternoon, I may stop again and wash the dishes real quick. Working like this is frustrating and counterproductive. By dividing attention between work and the house, I accomplish little in either area.

If you find it easy to work happily and productively in a state of disarray, congratulations. If you don't, make it a habit to pick up things before you begin working. I have found that if I take 30 minutes or so to straighten up in the morning, I get a lot more done during the day because I'm not wondering when I'll have time to get it done. I'm in a better state of mind because my work environment is more pleasant. Besides, if I'm more organized I'm also more productive. Establish a routine that works for *you.*

Even if your house is always as neat as a pin, you may find other things in your home distracting—the photographs under the bed that need organizing, the thank-you cards you need to get mailed, the grocery list that you need to write, etc. There are always little projects that need your attention at home. Working in the same place causes you to be reminded of them more than if you worked elsewhere. Heidi Haas, who runs a typesetting and design business from her home, says, "Juggling priorities is difficult. I have to stay motivated to go out and solicit business. Because I am home, I tend to see things around the house I need to do or things I want to do with my daughter." That is why it is so helpful to have a workplace in your home that is separated from family living areas. It's so much easier to forget about the mess or the projects if you can walk into your home office and shut the door. Even if you don't have a separate room in your home for your business, do as much as you can to make your work area separate.

Problem number 3: How in the world do you run a home business with children underfoot?

While having our children around is one of the benefits of home businesses, it is also a problem at times. There's no doubt that small children can make working at home a real challenge. This topic gets its own chapter! See Chapter 11: Where Do the Children Fit In? It is possible to combine your kids and your business successfully without going bonkers.

Problem number 4: You neglect your work because you find it difficult to alternate your mothering apron with your business hat.

It's easy to do, especially when you love your job of raising the precious little ones that God has given you. But if we spend all our time with the kids or let them and their schedules dictate our lives, we thwart our efforts at succeeding in our business. Heidi says, "It's easy to fall into being a mother and full-time homemaker and dropping the business because you are at home. You're not removed at an office, where you are away from everything. It's easy to get lazy in your business because you want to spend time with your family." Even without children, it can still be difficult to stick to your work when your spouse is around. If your mate is tending the barbecue while sipping a glass of lemonade or tea, or watching an old movie, it can be tough to concentrate on your task at hand.

The key here is to set hours for yourself and schedule your work time. One home-worker I know works best in the very early hours of the morning, before seeing to the needs of her family. Someone else may work best late at night, setting aside time to work after the kids are in bed. Whatever your schedule and work habits are, you will be more productive if you *schedule* time each week to get your work done. Then with work out of the way, you are free to enjoy your family.

Problem number 5: You lose valuable work time to outside forces.

The phone rings incessantly. The neighbors drop by. Friends ask favors of you since you're "home during the day." In general, people infringe on your time because you are in a home environment.

People working in an office environment have a built-in protection factor from such outside forces: secretaries, receptionists, and office buildings. Friends aren't as likely to call just to chat when they have to get past the front desk to get to you. The very nature of the office environment discourages a great many outside interruptions.

Working at home is so much "friendlier." People don't usually mean to disturb you, but often they don't understand that you do have to work even though you aren't in an office. They also don't know that their visit or phone call was ill-timed or one in a string of such interruptions.

Many home-workers solve this problem by setting business hours. They make sure that as many people as possible know the usual hours they work. If people know that you usually work in the mornings, or on Tuesdays and Wednesdays, or regular full-time business hours, chances are they'll try to honor your schedule, and you'll get more done. (Answering machines also solve a host of problems; more on that in a minute.)

Problem number 6: You chat too much with friends, make the refrigerator your constant companion, or are otherwise lacking in self-discipline.

Many people say they would have difficulty in working at home because they just couldn't stay away from their Kenmore double-doors. Others say they would talk on the phone too much, visit with their neighbors, or watch daytime TV. Those are valid concerns for many people, but the bottom line with all of those "work-stoppers" is a lack of discipline. You could padlock the fridge or throw out the TV, but if you don't have discipline in your life, working at home will be a source of frustration instead of the joy that it can be.

The Bible tells us to be disciplined. We must strive to achieve this character in our lives in order to be successful home-workers. "Listen to counsel and accept discipline, that you may be wise the rest of your days" (Proverbs 19:20).

Many home-workers identify some of the problem areas of working at home as snacking, sleeping late, watching TV, talking on the phone, talking with neighbors, reading, becoming too unprofessional, and procrastinating.

If you think that any of these or other temptations in your life might become a problem while working at home, ask the Lord to build the discipline in your life that is necessary to overcome this obstacle. Not only will this help you in your home business, but the overall quality of your life will improve as well. If a bad habit has become excessive in your life, recognize it as such. Knowing that you have a problem with food, TV, or whatever is often the first step toward solving it.

If you have trouble staying away from the kitchen, try scheduling snacks instead of waiting until the urge to eat hits you. (You'll eat healthier this way anyway.) Don't buy junk food, since it's much more tempting to grab a bag of chips to munch at your desk than it is to fix a healthy snack. If TV is a problem, try unplugging it during the day. If you have to go to the trouble of bending down to plug it in and then turn it on, you might stop the habit of just flicking the switch.

Develop good habits from the beginning. Learning to be disciplined in your life is much easier than trying to break a bad habit once it has developed.

Keeping Work from Invading Home Life

It's easy to let this problem get out of hand. Not long ago I had a zinger of a week. I made out my schedule in my trusty organizer with plenty of built-in "flextime." I knew what deadlines I had, what business desk-work I needed to tackle, what time to leave for my daughter's field trip, etc. What I hadn't planned on was the volume of interruptions. In four days eight people dropped by unexpectedly. Many of them stayed several hours. On one day alone I got over 20 phone calls. By the fifth day of this schedule, with work piling up, I was a bit agitated. I hadn't been able to finish the work I had wanted, my time with my family had been interrupted, and I was frustrated. I had to determine my problem and rethink how I could prevent this. It is too easy to let work dictate your family life.

Problem number 1: The phone keeps ringing.

What can you do? Two things: Buy an answering machine or get an answering service.

Answering machines are inexpensive and are a life-saver for the home-worker. When you are working and don't want to be interrupted you can let the machine take your calls. Or you can simply screen who you have time to talk to at that moment and then return the calls as soon as it is convenient for *you*. (You also don't have to miss business calls when you are seeing to the needs of your family.)

If you will be receiving a significant number of phone calls, a business line is a good idea. This way when the phone rings you know it's a business call and you can answer the phone with your business name. Also, after business hours you will know which calls are personal and which are business. If it's dinnertime with the family and the business line rings, let the machine get it or let it ring. If you want to be listed as a business with directory assistance or get a phone directory advertisement, you must have an official business line as the telephone company defines it. They will not sell you a yellow pages ad without the business line. (This is more costly than a residential line.) If you don't need the ad or the business listing, consider getting a second residential line as your business line.

Problem number 2: People needing your "business time" drop in, stay too long, and fragment your time.

There is a fine line between being flexible ("go with the flow") and allowing other people to dictate your schedule. Flexibility is important in a home business, but without any structure in your schedule you will find that you can be taken advantage of. To help solve this problem, learn to say no and to set business hours.

Saying no isn't always easy, but it will save you headaches in your business. I will confess that this has been hard for me to learn. When friends call and ask a favor, I want to be available to help them. Telling them no is often difficult, but sometimes necessary. When clients call and need "servicing," it's hard not to say yes immediately. One thing I have learned is to be stringent with my time. That is the most valuable commodity in any business—the owner's time. Instead of saying yes immediately when a client or friend calls asking for a favor or a meeting, *evaluate the timing*.

As Christians we are called to help meet the needs of others, to be Christlike in our family life, in our business life, and in our personal contacts. Meeting other people's needs, whether in the form of dropping everything and filling a rush order for a client or babysitting for a friend, sets a good example. Just remember to think through what you say yes to. If agreeing to a business meeting at 10:30 disrupts the timetable for the rest of your day, don't hesitate to suggest something that fits into your schedule. If your time is really short, let people know this, and suggest a starting and ending time for your meeting. They will respect you for your honesty. This is especially helpful if you have clients coming into your home.

Meetings with people outside your home also require tact if you feel they are going on too long and taking up too much of your time. But if these meetings are in your home, ending them can be difficult. You can't just walk out! If you set up a business meeting in your home, tell your clients in advance what time you have available. Try something like "John, I'd love to meet with you. How about Tuesday from 9:00 to 10:15?" If it's a personal visit that's keeping you from work, don't be afraid to let your visitor know that you must get back to your work. (Just do so with tact!)

If you have set hours (or if people at least think you do) it's easier to control your schedule instead of having it control you. When I first began my business I had a problem with clients calling or wanting to come by at all hours. Dinner with the family was frequently disturbed. I was called on weekends and late in the evenings. This was ruining my family time, and I felt like I never had any time off. I was always "on call" with my business. I finally learned to simply tell my clients my business hours and ask them to please call me or set appointments during those times. They didn't mind, and my family life improved drastically.

Problem number 3: Business visitors complicate your home life.

A trick that one home-worker uses is to encourage those who do business with her to drop off or pick up items even when she is not there. That allows her to continue to conduct business while she is away. I do this quite frequently myself. (Just agree on a safe place outside your home for the item to be left. One home-worker sets a box outside for her customers to drop off their work during her off hours. Be cautious, however, of potential problems like bad weather or theft.)

If business guests pose a problem at your home, try also doing business by mail, fax, telephone, or computer as often as possible. Offer to go to their location or to meet somewhere centrally located (perhaps a restaurant). Some of these situations may take you away from your home more often than you like, so determine what makes your home/work life easier for you.

Problem number 4: Deadlines rob you of family time.

This is one of the hardest problems to avoid in many businesses. Have the appliquéd garments delivered by March; deliver the brochure design by Tuesday; bake one case of cookies by noon. Even workers with traditional jobs struggle with deadlines.

How do you deal with deadlines?

1. Set hours.

2. Set priorities.

3. Know your limits.

4. Get outside help when needed.

Memorize these four steps and repeat them regularly, because they are easy to forget when the deadlines are tight.

For many businesses, setting hours will be enough. When the clock says it's quitting time, close your office door and be done. Other businesses must work on a tighter schedule which requires odd or extra hours. If that is the case, schedule the time you think the job will take when you agree to do the work.

Set priorities. Don't let the business conflict with the very reasons you started your business. Don't let the pursuit of money color your vision for your family. The Bible cautions us against being purely money-motivated: "Do not weary yourself to gain wealth; cease from your consideration of it" (Proverbs 23:4). It's easy to let the workload get out of hand, especially in a growing business. Just remember your priorities and why you wanted to work at home in the first place.

Know your limits in the amount of work you can take on. There's nothing worse than taking on more work than you can handle if there's no one available to help when you need it, or if it's badly timed with other commitments you have. Don't promise more than you can deliver even if you have to turn down work. Overload can be a major source of home-business stress.

When you take on more work than you can handle in the given amount of time to meet your deadline, get outside help. The help may just be temporary to get you through the tough spot, but if your business is growing to the point that outside help is necessary, don't delay in getting help. It could mean the difference between business growth and business failure.

Business help can come from a number of sources. Try recruiting the kids. Hiring them will not only help you, but will teach your children a great many things as well. You could also hire an outsider. Be careful to check your zoning regulations, since they often prohibit workers who do not live at your residence from working in your home business. (If they do prohibit that and if you have the room, look into a live-in employee. It's a possible solution for some.)

You will save yourself headaches and endless paperwork if you do not need a regular worker. That person can then be a contract worker for you instead of an employee.

Have your spouse join you full-time in the business. The number of couples engaged in business together at home is growing. There are numerous family advantages to this arrangement and you also have the opportunity for more business growth.

You can also barter help with friends or business associates or check into contract service employees or temporary help.

Problem number 5: Your work is cluttering your home.

If you can't find the dining room table or walk through the bedroom because of your work paraphernalia, it's time to get organized and try to separate your work physically from the areas of your home you *live* in.

Leaving craft supplies or computer equipment on the kitchen table means they have to be moved before dinner can be served. You and your family will quickly tire of this hassle and of seeing the mess. You will also feel like you are never away from the business if it is constantly around you. Separate your family life from your business life physically in whatever way you can.

It is important to define your workspace. If that is a separate room, it's simple. When you shut the office door you are in your work environment. If you do not have a separate room for your office, borrow space from an existing room. *Home Offices and Workspaces* also suggests hallways, staircase landings, and under-the-stairway areas for possible work areas. With proper lighting and ventilation, even a small closet can become an office. Just be sure your work area is defined. Even if you are creating an office at home where no room exists, separate that area with some sort of physical barrier.

Another way to keep your work separate from the family is to establish house rules. When you first begin your business, discuss with your family what the ground rules will be. For example, I have tried to establish the rule with my children that when Mommy's door is shut that means she is working. What noise level will you allow? It's important to let your children know what you expect in this regard. Will you allow them to bring toys into your work area? What are the house rules when business visitors arrive? Knowing the rules in advance makes combining your work and your family easier.

Another good way to keep your work from invading your home is to keep all your supplies, equipment, current projects, and files in one location. If you spread them out in your home you have a tendency to be more disorganized. If you keep everything together you will be able to find things faster and easier without having to hunt for them or trek across the house when you need an item not at your desk. Also, your family will know to stay out of your things if all of your work is in one location. It's much easier to explain to the kids "This area is Mommy's office; please don't touch anything in here" than it is to say "Don't touch the things in the corner, on the top of the dryer, or on the workbench in the garage."

Problem number 6: Breaks are few and far between.

By living and working in the same place you can often get the feeling that you are never away from your work. This can lead to long hours and bad habits. People who work for themselves often have a tendency to work harder than if they were working for someone else. If you have to, force yourself to stop and take a break or eat a meal if you are prone to work through lunch or dinner. One home-worker said, "I make myself stop and eat regularly when I'm working, even if I just stop for 20 minutes. That way I feel better and I'm more productive. Office workers take lunch hours, so we should too."

If you don't control the amount of time you spend in your business, it will begin to control you. Never forget that your family needs your time too.

Tips to Keep Home Life from Invading Work

- Be organized in your home.
- Delegate.
- Separate yourself mentally from things in your home.
- Straighten up before beginning work.
- Separate your physical work area.
- Set house rules with your family.
- Set business hours.
- Schedule time each week for your home responsibilities.
- Limit TV.
- Schedule snack/meal breaks.
- Pray for and develop discipline.

Tips to Keep Work from Invading Home Life

- Be organized in your work.
- Get an answering machine or service.
- Get a business line.
- Learn to say no.
- Set business hours.
- Set start/end times for meetings.
- Encourage others to drop off or pick up while you are away.
- Conduct business by mail/fax/computer whenever possible.
- Get outside help when you need it.
- Know your work limits.
- Set priorities.
- Have a separate work area.
- Keep your work materials in one location.

Some of the problems that keep you from working in your business are also the same problems that keep you from enjoying your home life. You need to make a conscious effort to protect your home life from an all-out invasion by your business life.

8
Managing Your Business

One popular book identified the keys to success for some of the top companies in the world. These companies had one thing in common: They were brilliant on the basics and kept things simple in a complex world. To successfully manage a home business you must keep the way you manage your business as simple and basic as possible, but do so intelligently. To be a successful home-worker you must manage your paperwork, money, time, and home. In this chapter we'll talk about keeping track of your paperwork and your money. To do that you must begin with the basics—an organized and workable system.

Organize, Organize, Organize!

It's been said that disorganization causes 80 percent of overcrowding. Think about it—if you clean out your messy, crowded coat closet you do two things: You throw out what you don't need and you organize what you do need. And when you're finished you usually have more room for the family coats! Author Emilie Barnes has a complete home-maintenance system built around that principle. The same principle needs to be applied to your business as well. Organize, and toss out the unessential.

Use whatever gimmicks help you successfully organize the necessities of your business: files, business cards, addresses, phone numbers, computer disks, canceled checks, magazines, and any other paperwork your business generates. Go to a large office supply store and discover what is available (you might be surprised at the variety). Determine what you have in your office that needs organizing, and then purchase or make an appropriate storage system.

Business cards can be stored on Rolodex cards, in a "business card holder" with plastic sleeves, or in other ways.

Addresses, phone numbers, and business cards can be organized in Rolodex boxes or rings, address books, or card files. Be sure to keep this information near the phone for easy access where you will use it. Also be sure to have some type of phone message system near your phone. A bound message book works best because you will always have a record to refer to if you should need it (rather than "Post-Its," pink slips, or scratch paper).

Check your computer store for different types of computer disk storage. Such systems come in flat containers, upright models, and plastic or wooden boxes. Always remember to keep a record of your file titles, since it can be easy to forget what you named a particular document. (There are computer programs that do this for you as well.) Instead of keeping your files on your disks in chronological order, try labeling disks for each type of file that you might have, such as projects, clients, invoices, programs, etc.

Files can be stored in purchased filing cabinets (cardboard, metal, or wood), old moving boxes, or even in orange crates. Stationery stores carry cardboard boxes made just for storing canceled checks and back issues of magazines. Bookshelves can be anything from hand-rubbed oak to plywood and cinder blocks. The more organized you are in storing your business information, the faster and easier you can find what you need when you need it.

A Filing System

Setting up an efficient, workable, and well-organized filing system is vital to your business management. Many people recommend the basic Pendaflex system that's available in letter or legal size from most office supply and discount department stores. Larger hanging file folders hold manila folders with more specific headings.

When setting up your filing system, determine which files are most important. Which files get used the most? Those are the ones that need to be kept in the front of the filing cabinet. You should be able to find everything in a minute or two. Many people prefer to alphabetize even the hanging files, but if the set of files you use most often is in the back of your file cabinet, it becomes more difficult to reach them in a hurry or when you are on the phone. Instead, alphabetize the individual manila file folders within the division file folders.

You might set your files up with clear, specific headings such as: Projects (particular jobs), Clients (particular people), General Business (filed by subjects, such as "Couriers," "Laser Printer," etc.), Correspondence, Finances ("Paid Bills," "Accounts Receivable," etc.), and Futures. These headings can be put on the file section folders, which are available in different colors for coding the different sections of your filing system.

A futures file (sometimes called a tickler file) is used in the news business to keep track of events and stories that are upcoming, but it can be useful in a home business as well. Take 31 manila file folders and label each consecutively 1 to 31. As you process your mail or note an upcoming event or project, put the information in the file with the corresponding date, always keeping that day's file in the front. Each morning check that file and put it in the back when you are through. You may want to check the next day's date in the evening to help you plan your day. If you get a flier on a seminar you want to attend on the 15th, put it in the folder labeled "15," in addition to marking your appointment book or calendar. This system enables you to not only keep up with your appointments and projects but also to know where the corresponding information about each thing is. You can locate that information in seconds.

Don't leave files lying around in your "file pile"; use it or lose it. When your files begin to get crowded, sort through them and remove the inactive files to a storage box. My filing system got so packed at one point (because I failed to purge the old files) that I could hardly get any of the files in or out. That wastes time and efficiency.

Record-Keeping

Keeping accurate records is very important for two simple reasons: 1) Without them you won't know if you are making or losing money, and 2) without them you won't get all the tax deductions to which you are entitled. A good bookkeeping system is the key to your company's fiscal health. You do not need to have an accounting background to set up and keep good books.

Keep everything related to your business finances, and file it as you get it. Believe it or not, some people have actually thrown out their bank statements because they didn't think they needed to keep them. People are often intimidated at tax time and put off preparing their taxes because they have not kept accurate records. If you keep up with your record-keeping as you go along, you will be ready and waiting when the tax man cometh. You will also be a better business manager, since keeping good records is the key to knowing how you are doing.

For some people it's the lack of know-how or not valuing the importance of a system that keeps them from having accurate records.

I fell into that category when I first started my business. I am the sort of person who likes to have a calculator for any and all math functions and would rather have my teeth drilled than learn accounting. I'm not a sloppy person by any means and in fact am fairly well-organized; it's just that I have this crazy aversion to numbers. Therefore when I first began my business I had a tough row to hoe. While I was still learning what record-keeping was, my husband proceeded to set me straight. He handed me a set of papers with columns printed on them and headings like "receivables" and "expenses," and then told me to record everything for the past three months, since he couldn't make heads or tails of my records. Boy, was that fun! I thought I had my own system, but obviously it wasn't working very well.

Since my husband also happens to be my own personal accountant, he determined to teach me a little about keeping good records. By having my own live-in CPA I had no choice but to get past my irrational fear of numbers and accounting lingo. By the very nature of my character I will never decide to join my husband in opening up a computer bookkeeping service, but I have learned a great deal about the importance of being organized and up-to-date in keeping records.

A good friend of mine started her own business from her home, and before she had been operational for even two days she had reams of paperwork filed neatly in a notebook. I must say it took me a bit longer to learn this skill than it did for her, but the point is that if I can, anyone can.

A Record-Keeping System

Most home-business owners keep their accounting system simple, do it themselves, and are not necessarily computerized. A variety of simple bookkeeping systems can be purchased at your local office supply store. For those who already own computers, several accounting packages are available at modest prices to make keeping records and compiling monthly reports as easy as possible.

To keep track of all of your expenses and income and to be sure you get it all recorded in your books, try this easy-to-use system. Label two large envelopes Business Income and Business Expenses. Put them somewhere with easy access in your work area. Try taping them up near your desk or tacking them to the wall or on a bulletin board. These envelopes will help you keep track of all records in these two categories.

Business Income: In this envelope keep copies of all checks, receipts of all sales, or bank deposit slips that list the name or number of the check. In other words, keep a record of all business income.

Business Expenses: In this envelope keep receipts (even handwritten ones) for every penny you spend on your business, stubs from paid business bills, or canceled checks which you wrote for business expenses.

At the end of the month tally the envelopes. It's easy to see just how much you spent in each category and how much you received as income. Keep each month's records stapled together in their respective envelopes, so that determining the quarterly or year-to-date figures is easy. This system makes it easy to keep your income and expense information organized and your business records up-to-date. If you fall behind in entering your records into your bookkeeping system, it is simple to catch up. You don't have to scrounge around trying to find invoices here and receipts there to make your journal entries. If properly used, this method becomes a habit. Whether your record-keeping system is done by hand or is computerized, keep it up-to-date.[1]

Always separate your business and personal finances. By doing this you will be able to more easily see where you stand financially in your business each month, budgeting will be simpler, and tax time will be easier because your records will be clearer.

Keeping Track of Expenses

It is easy to lose track of expenses if you lose track of your receipts. Many home businesses begin spending money for the business before they have a business account. A business expense is easier to lose that way, and since most such expenses are tax-deductible, you won't want to miss a single one. One simple way to be sure you keep all records is to carry one of your business envelopes in your purse or wallet. When you are out and find that you have made a purchase that is business-related, at the time of the purchase put the receipt in that envelope. When you get home, put it in the appropriate larger envelope.

Another thing you won't want to neglect is recording your auto mileage. You will want to keep accurate records of the miles you put on the family car while you are out and about for business purposes. This may be an automatic procedure for you, but it was tough for me to remember to do at first. It seemed like I was always in a hurry and never remembered to write down my mileage or car expenses when I got home. Sometimes I would write it down on gas tickets, grocery bags, or whatever else was handy. This record-keeping was just a hodge-podge. Often I thought I had recorded everything, but when I looked at my record at the end of the month, I knew I had driven more business miles than I had recorded. So I bought a little 49-cent spiral notebook (or you can purchase an auto mileage book) and a small pen which I inserted in the spiral binding. I attached it to my sun visor and made it a habit to never get out of the car without writing down the mileage *right then*. I developed another habit: Before I get out of the car I zero out my trip odometer. (If your car has this feature, use it!) Then when I get in the car I don't have to think about the number of miles on the odometer, nor do I have to subtract from the mileage when I finish driving. I only have to think about my mileage once—when I get home and before I get out of the car. I look at the trip odometer, record it in my spiral book, zero out the counter so I'm ready for my next trip, and I'm done. It takes only seconds each time, but it's a good system and I'm always up-to-date.

There are all kinds of books and resources available for the specific how-to's of good record-keeping for the small business owner. More important than the type of system you have is the fact that you have a system at all.

Some people say that if you spend over half an hour a day for business finances, it is time to get help. You can hire a part-time bookkeeper or an accountant, or you can computerize your accounting system, depending on the size of your business and your needs.

Better Business Management

- Know where you stand each month.
  Balance your account. Know your true balance at all times. Check your envelopes and sort them.

- Know your expenses.
  Where is all of your money going each month?

- Know what bills you owe.
  Record them daily as they come in. Know when they are due.

- Know where all your records are.
  File them as you get them. Make this a
  habit. Be able to find receipts, work orders,
  client files, and payment information within three minutes.
- Know where everything is.
  Make sure your filing system is well-organized.
- Know the time you have invested.
  You will know if you are being productive.
  If you aren't productive, you can work to
  improve. You must also know your time if
  you bill clients or customers for it. Do this
  daily.
- Know your inventory.
  Check this daily. What products do you
  have on hand? What supplies? Know what
  you've sold and the amount of sales tax
  you've collected, if necessary. Keep a log
  and control your inventory. Don't let your
  supplies run too low, so you won't be
  caught unable to fill an order or do a job. I
  once got a large volume of laser printing
  for a client. About halfway through the
  printing my toner cartridge ran out. To
  give the client his work when I had promised, I had to purchase a new cartridge at
  more than double what I normally pay. (It
  takes several days to get them at my lower
  rate.) By not keeping track of the condition
  of my supplies, I got low on a business
  commodity and had to pay for my over-
  sight.
- Know your invoicing status.
  Do this daily or weekly, depending on your
  business. I invoice as I finish a job. That

way I never have to wonder if I did it. If invoicing is done in a timely fashion, you won't miss out on money owed to you because of sloppy record-keeping.

About Your Money

Don't plan on making a profit for the first few months. Most traditional businesses plan on operating in the red for the first couple of years. However, because you are operating your business from your home with little overhead, you should normally expect to see a profit before that long a time. By carefully managing your money and periodically evaluating your financial condition, you will see your profit as quickly as possible.

Small-business financial consultant Vera Peirsol of Vapco Services, Inc. (herself home-based), recommends doing a profit-and-loss statement at the end of every month, or at least at the end of each quarter. This helps you compare how you are doing with your budget. Comparing what you have made with what you have spent each month will give you a clear understanding of how healthy your business is.

Looking at these financial reports will also help in preparing financial projections for the future. After the first three months, take a good long look at your balance sheet. Compare your profit-and-loss statement and your expenditures with your budget. Determine if you need to be spending more or less in any area. Do you need to add a business phone line, buy more equipment, hire some additional help, reduce inventory or supplies, or produce more or less advertising? Evaluate these things and estimate how much you think you will grow in the coming months. When you forecast your financial growth you are creating a target. Without a business target to shoot for, you will stay where you are or be ill-prepared to handle growth.

To realize a profit as soon as possible in your business and continue to be prosperous, remember two important rules: 1) Don't spend money you haven't earned, and 2) control your costs! It's so easy to get in debt but so difficult to get out. There are some situations where business debt might be advised, but don't get yourself in any more of a financial bind than necessary. One person I interviewed explained how she kept costs down and learned to trust God for her business at the same time. "I didn't hire a delivery service. I got a pizza delivery guy to make my deliveries in his spare time at a fraction of the cost. I didn't get slick, glossy, beautiful labels for my products printed right off the bat, but instead used mailing labels. You have to be real humble. I intend to have a refrigerated delivery truck, my own bakery, and the slick, glossy labels in the future, but people often put out a lot of money and then they're bound to their businesses. For me, the Lord can't work as well then because it's harder to listen with creditors at my door. On the other hand, I have to be willing to let go of dollars when necessary. It's a matter of balance."

Are You Managing Your Money Properly?

You will be if you remember these points:

- Know your bank balance.
- Pay your bills on time.
- Invoice each week.
- Control your costs.
- Try to earn money before you spend it.
- Know where your money is going.

Cash Flow

Simply defined, cash flow is cash receipts less cash

expenses for any given period. Hopefully you'll get that check that's "in the mail" before your bills come due! To have a healthy cash flow, you must continue to generate new business and collect on that business as soon as you can. That's the bottom line. To help alleviate cash-flow problems, consider the following points:

- Aim for COD (cash on delivery) for services or products whenever possible.

- When you take on new business (particularly if you are a service business), get a percentage down in advance, thereby providing you with operating capital.

- Bill out at least every 30 days.

- Offer a discount to your customers if they pay your invoice within ten days of the date of the statement. One home-business owner who did this said, "Eighty percent of my billings are in by the 10th or 15th of the month since I began to offer the discount. I usually have a 100 percent collection rate every month. If I don't, the client knows I don't work for him the next month until I get paid."

- Have "Payment Due Upon Receipt" printed on every invoice.

- Get credit from your suppliers. If you can get a 10, 30 or even 60-day net with some suppliers, you will do a lot toward minimizing cash-flow difficulties.

- Prioritize your bills. Know which bills are the most important. First pay the debts that are collateralized. If you don't make your house payment, they can take your house, etc. Next pay your utilities. If you don't have electricity or a phone, you can't run your business.

Third, pay your suppliers. If you don't have supplies and a good relationship with them, doing business will be very difficult.

- Deal with your creditors honestly. Never say the check is in the mail if it isn't. If you plan on paying a business bill after a certain check comes in and that client doesn't pay you on time, call your creditor and tell him the situation. Instead of this forthrightness hurting your credibility, he or she will probably respect you for being honest. We are subject to a higher authority anyway, so operating honestly should be second nature to Christian business people.

- Project your cash flow between the 1st and the 15th, then determine your bills due during that time. Do the same for the remainder of the month. If you don't have enough billed out to meet that month's obligations, let your creditors know this, and ask them for an extension. Or get your suppliers to give you terms for 60 days. If the imbalance continues, you need to get serious about increasing your monthly billings. Generate more cash! Market, market, market for new business.

Tips for Good Business Organization

- Write your business plan.

- Have organized files.

- Have a good record-keeping system and use it diligently.

- Evaluate your monthly expenses against your business budget.

- Maintain your cash flow. Keep tabs on your monthly income compared to your business bills.

- Evaluate your financial reports monthly.

- Forecast financial growth.

Letting Others Know About Your Product/Service

No matter how good your product is, or how professional your service is, no one is going to buy it unless they know about it. No one is going to know about it unless you tell them. Telling as many people about your business as possible and promoting those people to do business with you is the name of the sales game. Marketing if you will.

Marketing is simply your company's advertising, promotion (including publicity which is free promotion), and sales efforts. Estimate early in your business (and continue to reevaluate) what your advertising needs are and how you can reach your consumers or clients. If you sell a product determine if you will be in retail sales (direct to consumers, but not usually workable for home businesses), mail order sales, or wholesale sales (to distributors who in turn sell to the consumer). Each approach involves a different sales and marketing approach. There are many, many books available to help you market your business. Spend some time researching how to pitch your product or sell your service. Remember, your cash flow depends on it.

To Insure That You Are Paid

Try to protect yourself in advance against collection difficulties by using a financial agreement, preferably written rather than verbal. Such an agreement is basically a contract of terms and is highly recommended, especially in service businesses. Have one basic agreement for which you can fill in the blanks for each client. Include:

1. The details of the job.

2. Payment arrangements.

3. Hourly rate or base price.

4. Special terms (such as 50 percent down, 50 percent upon completion).

5. Start and completion dates.

6. Signatures of you and your client.

Have your customer sign the agreement and give him a copy, keeping one for yourself.

What to Do if Clients Won't Pay

Reinvoice them with a past-due notice in bold print on the bill. If they still don't pay within ten days, call them and ask when you can expect payment. If they are having difficulties or owe on a current and past invoice, arrange a payment plan with them to assure them that you are willing to negotiate. If you show that you are willing to work with them, they will be more likely to pay you. If you suspect, however, that your client is a deadbeat, get tough! You don't need that kind of client in the first place.

A friend of mine who is a soft-spoken, mild-mannered woman is excellent at collections. Once a company gave her trouble in paying her invoice. After gentle reminders, she visited their office and threatened to drive up and down the street with a sign on her car proclaiming, "X Company owes me $2000 and won't pay!" Needless to say, she left that day with her check. Several weeks later the company folded, but she got her money!

Another tactic is to call and ask when your check will be ready, then tell them you will be by in person to pick it up. If they say it's not ready when you get there, tell them you'll wait!

Collection agencies and small claims court are a last resort.

Networking

One of the buzzwords in business these days is networking. Networking is simply making as many contacts as possible with other people for your benefit and theirs. It's making contact with people you don't know. Networking can be important for the home-business person, since he is removed from a social work environment.

If others know you run an "xyz" business, they may call *you* when they need "xyz." Both parties can benefit. For example, through networking I discovered several other people in my area who were in the same type of business as I am. I have been able to hire them when I have an overflow of work. When they are booked, they can call on me. Use networking if you are looking to share part-time help. Home-workers have been able to share part-time secretaries for their business, or even household help by finding other home-workers with similar needs. Check your phone book for networking clubs in your area, and be sure to let your friends and new acquaintances know about your business.

Bartering

Check your phone directory for bartering clubs in your area. They can save you money and provide goods or services that you might not otherwise be able to afford. Even if you do not join a club, you might be surprised at the number of people who are open to barter services. I designed an advertising flier for a company in exchange for their referral service and we both saved money. The IRS has specific rules about bartering in terms of taxable income and deductible expenses, so be sure to check with your accountant first. Keep records of any bartering in which you engage.

One woman in Massachusetts who runs a home-based word-processing business depleted her resources in the beginning with a $20,000 investment in home office equipment.[2] Many people would never be able to start home businesses without some creative ways to come up with the needed resources and equipment. Bartering can offer the solution in some instances.

Home-worker Angela Kopenan bartered her typesetting services in exchange for the equipment she needed. "I was fortunate. I was able to purchase my laser equipment because a client financed it in exchange for work I did for her. That led to other word-of-mouth jobs." The client was happy because Angela provided her with a needed service. Angela was thrilled since it gave her a means to start her own business with very little capital.

That is the very way I started my own business. I was the managing editor of a trade publication, and I designed and typeset the magazine on my employer's computer. I knew I wanted a computer of my own, so my employer financed one for me. We just deducted the monthly cost of the computer from the income I received for editing and laying out the magazine. In a short time I owned my own equipment, which enabled me to take on other jobs and eventually start my own business from my home. I was able to start small, without depleting my resources or getting a loan, by using a type of barter arrangement. The company provided what I needed and I provided a service for them.

Managing your own business need not be as intimidating as some people think. Organize your business information, keep accurate records, and stay on top of your finances. If you do those three things, you will be on your way to a prosperous and well-managed home business. But don't stop there; remember to take your business problems to the Lord. He cares very much about the details in our lives and earnestly desires to lead us. We should strive to become excellent business managers as we seek direction and wisdom from the Lord.

"The mind of man plans his way, but the Lord directs his steps" (Proverbs 16:9).

9

Managing Your Time

Why is it that some people can climb mountains while others struggle with molehills? One of the biggest reasons is *time management*. Those who succeed in getting a lot done use each hour to their advantage. They are thrifty with their time—they carefully consider how they spend it. Those who are left in the dust midway up their molehills usually don't evaluate whether they are using their time effectively. Many people simply do not know how to manage their day.

Stacy described her surprise at the difficulty in managing her time with a home business. "It's harder to get things done than I ever thought it would be. It takes more phone calls, more looking for things, and just more time to get things accomplished." When Mike was asked what he wished he had known when he first started his business, his response was, "Just how much time running a business from home really takes. I had to learn through trial and error just how much time everything takes. I needed to do some preplanning to figure out how to make it all work for me. I wish I had worked out a time-management strategy before I jumped into it."

Since the timing of almost everything you do in your day builds on the activity just preceding it, you get a kind of snowball effect. If you wake up late and have a full day planned, you're off to a bad start. If you have to pick up the cleaning by 5:00, but your 4:00 o'clock meeting ran too long, you had better plan on wearing something else tomorrow. Not only that, but things usually take twice as long as you think they will. A two-hour job can easily turn into four hours, counting interruptions. To better gauge how much time things will really take, make a list of all your projects or activities and estimate how long you think each will take. Then at the end of the day write down how long they actually took. Chances are that you probably underestimated.[1] Learning how to properly estimate the time needed to complete your tasks is one of the most vital keys to effectively using your time.

Time management has even become big business. There are all kinds of systems on the market, from "daytimers" to diskettes, from workshops to workbooks, to help us manage our time effectively. For the home-business person, managing how you spend your day is critical. You need to get mileage out of your minutes! How can you do that? Be organized. Be flexible. Schedule your time. Don't procrastinate. And dedicate each day to the Lord.

Be Organized

Just as it is important to be organized in the way you manage your business, so it is important to be organized in how you manage your time.

1. *Use an organization system.* Many people are good list-makers, writing down what they must do each day, but with a home business demanding your time and attention, a more detailed organizational system could serve you well. Instead of having various notes or lists lying around the house, try using an organizer. There are many different types available from office supply stores and department stores. You can even make your own with a three-ring binder and notebook paper. The basics include the following categories: a yearly, monthly,

and weekly calendar; things to do today; and an address/ phone number list. You might also want to include a section for current and long-range goals. You can also personalize your organizer for your lifestyle, preferences, and particular home business. Then you have in one location your list for what to do today, tomorrow, next week, and next month. Combining your "to-do list" with your appointment diary, calendar, and address book can save you much time.

If you own a personal computer, time-management programs are available for it. One home-business owner told me he uses a program that not only lets him list his daily activities, appointments, and so forth, but that also alerts him when it is time for a particular thing by sounding an alarm. My mother always leaves herself notes on the refrigerator to remind her of upcoming events and appointments. If she forgets to check her calendar, she'll remember when she makes her next meal. *No matter what type of gadget you prefer to keep you organized and on time, use one to your advantage.*

2. *Set goals.* If you want to accomplish something, set a goal. Some studies have said that those who write down their goals are 90 times more likely to accomplish them than those who don't. Write down your daily, weekly, monthly, and yearly goals—what you want to accomplish in that given time period. You can even go a step further: Write down your medium-range and long-range goals as well. But don't stop there. Also write down the steps you will need to take to make your goal a reality—a road map, if you will, to your destination.

If your daily goal is to get one new client, your action plan could show that you must call five new prospects. If your daily goal is to finish your current project, your action plan would show that you must type ten pages, or bake seven dozen muffins, or whatever specific steps are necessary to accomplish that goal. This goal-setting action-plan idea works for small daily tasks as well as for long-range goals. If you want to build a country home, start a second business, or go into business with your spouse, write down what you need to do in order to accomplish that goal along with a timetable for getting it done. After all, goals are just dreams with deadlines.[2]

3. *Prioritize your activities.* After writing down what you must do, the next step is to determine the order of importance of the things on that list. What absolutely *must* be done before the day is over? What would you *like* to have done? What could possibly wait until tomorrow? Give your list a 1, 2, 3 . . . rating and tackle each item in the appropriate order. If you get to the end of the list, great! If you get to the end of the day first, move your unaccomplished objectives to the top of your list for tomorrow.

Be Flexible

When considering how to manage your time with a home business, one of the most sanity-saving tidbits to remember is *be flexible!* Working where you live mandates a certain level of flexibility, or else you will be tried beyond belief. Children, telephones, doorbells, housework, and neighbors can make it nearly impossible to get things done at times. If you had planned on working at your desk from 2:00 to 5:00, but at 2:45 your washing machine overflows, you have to shift your plans. If you were to work at an "outside" job, you wouldn't even have known about the problem until you walked in the door at the end of the day. But when you're at home you can't just slosh through the mess. You stop what you're doing, clean it up, and finish your work at another time.

The flip side of that is being flexible for the fun things as well. Occasionally you may have your day planned, but a friend calls and says, "If you come over right now you

can meet the President," or, "My uncle loaned me his cata-
maran today. Do you want to go for an afternoon sail?"
A steady diet of abandoning scheduled work for a day of
fun can lead to an unhealthy business, but being flexible enough to occasionally enjoy a spur-of-the-moment
activity is one of the reasons people work from their
homes.

Schedule Your Time

1. *Schedule time for paperwork.* Set aside a certain time
each day or week to do your paperwork. File your receipts. Invoice your clients. Balance your account. Pay
your bills. Don't wait until the bank is calling, your
creditors are knocking, and your in-box is overflowing.
Schedule time *daily or weekly* to tend to your paperwork,
depending on the size and nature of your business. Put it
on your calendar if you have to.

2. *Don't fragment your time.* One way to make the most
of your time is to divide your day into similar things by
category. Group all your phone calls, projects, and errands
to be done at the same time.

Organize your business tasks with your household
tasks if they are in the same category. Since you work at
home there is no need to keep business and personal
activities separated during your day. You don't have to
wait until 5:00 to stop for milk. You can do it on the way
to the office supply store, or along with other business
errands.

Plan to do your phone-calling in the morning. It is
easier to catch people this way. Plan your errands during non-rush-hour times (another home-working perk).
Group your errands by proximity. Think it through
before you go. Order your errands not just by what must
be done first, but along the shortest route as well.

It wastes time and is unproductive to shift to and from
various modes throughout the day. While you should

always try to group similar things together, try to finish doing one thing before you shift to another. I may be in the mommy mode, wife mode, business professional mode, and homemaker mode throughout a given day. I like to try to group activities in these different modes together. If I'm going to be making sales calls, cookies, and carpool runs, I try to do similar things together. For me it is much more enjoyable to finish all my work, then have undisturbed time with my family. By grouping my activities I save start-and-stop time, and my leisure time is in larger segments as well.

3. *Work at the time that is most productive for you.* Determine when you are most productive. When do you have the most energy? When do you think most clearly? What time of day do you most like to work? When do you get sleepy or sluggish? Evaluate these factors in light of your family's schedule. Strive to work during your peak performance period if that does not conflict too much with the routine of your family.

4. *Set some type of routine.* You do not have to be limited to the nine-to-five routine (or the "Sesame Street" to "Mr. Rogers' Neighborhood" schedule!). Whether you have come from the corporate world or the "kiddie corner," set up some type of routine that works for you. Even people who hate routine can benefit from some semblance thereof. If you plan a time to work, you will accomplish more in that given period than if you just work when you are so moved.

Some people make the most efficient use of their time by working traditional nine-to-five hours in their home office. Others like to work in their businesses part of the day and in their homes the other part. Still others establish a routine of working in the business on certain days only, and taking off several days during the week. Many

businesses tend to be seasonal, with longer hours required during holidays, tax time, etc.

If you like a lot of structure in your life and don't have
children, you may want to stick to traditional office
hours. If you have school-age children, try to get the bulk
of your work done before 3:00 in the afternoon. If you
hate routine, working at home gives you the option of
working hard for several days and then taking some
time off. Whatever routine you choose, and how rigid
you make it, is entirely up to you. Just establishing a goal
of when you will try to work at home leads to a more
effective use of your time.

5. *Be selective in what you take on.* If you say yes to a
friend, a project, or a job, consider how that decision will
affect you in the coming hours, days, or weeks. Do you
have enough time to fulfill your obligation without having it complicate other things in your schedule? This
one's hard for me. I tend to say yes too readily, then
realize after I'm in the middle of things that I haven't
planned my time properly to finish my obligations.
Before you commit to things, be sure you look at how
they will affect you, your family, and your other time
commitments. I am still working on this one!

6. *Backtime when scheduling your activities.* List all the
things you want to accomplish. Then list the amount of
time you think it will take to accomplish each thing.
Count backward from the time you need to be done. If
you have a project that is due by next week, figure out
how many days you have left to accomplish your task.
Divide the steps necessary to meet that goal into daily
assignments until your project is complete or your deadline has been met. Don't just work on a project blind to
your time frame. Whether it's a month-long project or an
hourlong task, know where you need to be at any given
point.

7. *Schedule extra time.* When making your schedule, plan for flextime. Give yourself some padding in your appointments and activities. Figure extra time into your schedule. You will occasionally get lost. The baby will sometimes spit up on you as you are walking out the door. You may get in your car and find that the gas gauge is on "empty." If you have some padding in your time schedule, you can meet these minor inconveniences without having them become major dilemmas. Don't book your schedule too tightly. If you schedule an extra 15 minutes between appointments, and nothing goes wrong, you will be early. That's much better than having no time cushion, then encountering a problem and arriving late and frazzled.

8. *When scheduling meetings, evaluate their importance.* Is this meeting really necessary? Many of them waste time because you could just as easily accomplish the same thing by phone, mail, fax, or modem. Remember, don't hesitate to set the length of a meeting in advance or end a meeting that is dragging. Unproductive meetings are big time robbers.

Some meetings can be unproductive but you don't mind—if they are with people you want to be with, and you also have the time. This is one way to avoid the isolation problem that some home-workers experience. However, if you would rather spend your time with someone else, or if time is short, decide whether you must actually meet with him or her in person.

9. *Ask how you should spend your time.* Some experts say that you should spend 50 percent of your time making your product or providing your service, 25 percent of your time marketing your business, and 25 percent of your time running your business.[3] Other sources say that entrepreneurs actually spend their business time in

keeping records, direct selling, production, maintenance, dealing with suppliers, arranging financial matters, planning, and dealing with employees.

A survey done by the National Federation of Independent Businesses found that a majority of people who start a small business do so during the years that many people start their families. Sixty percent began their companies from the ages of 25 to 40, and many owners work as many as 60 or 70 hours a week, especially when the businesses are young.[4] The business may be young at this time, but often so are the children, so be thoughtful in the amount of time you allot to each.

Just as you should carefully consider how to spend your time, also consider how *not* to spend your time. Are there things you are spending time on that are not productive, or that do not contribute to your personal, family, or spiritual life? First let's consider television. It's a simple fact—people who watch a lot of TV cannot accomplish what they could if they limited their viewing. Television has been accused of being the great national babysitter, the roadblock to literacy, the undermining of the family, and one of the greatest time-wasters known to man. It desensitizes us, stifles our creativity, thwarts our imagination, robs us of personal communication, and negatively influences us in a number of ways. Many people are opting to pitch the set entirely! One family described what happened when they drastically limited the amount of television in their home: "After three months my wife and I began to see things happen. Suddenly we had the time each night as a family to read aloud, to read to ourselves, to do homework at an unhurried pace, to learn how to play chess and checkers . . . to draw and paint and color, and—best of all—to talk with each other, asking questions and answering questions. Our children's imaginations were coming back to life again."[5]

It's hard to hear that still, small voice of God when the TV is blaring. One author, a simple country preacher, said that he felt God guiding him to give up the two hours of TV he watched at night after the kids were in bed. Instead, he spent that time in prayer. Shortly after making that decision, and during that time with the Lord, he felt God guiding him in some specific ways. That night played an important part in the ministry of David Wilkerson, author and founder of Teen Challenge.

Even though there are some good entertaining and educational programs on television, and my children are familiar with "Bert" and "Ernie," there have been times when I wished the thing would blow up. More important, however, is to learn to control the monster in our living rooms instead of allowing it to control us.

When you have a home business, time is very limited. Television can be a great time thief if you allow it to be.

Tips to Controlling Your Television

- Move it out of the living room.
- Don't let it be the focal point of the room.
- Put it in a cabinet with doors.
- Keep it unplugged.
- Determine a time limit for your own viewing and your children's.
- Keep alternative entertainment sources handy, making it easy to grab something besides the "on" switch.

10. *Get your family's cooperation.* If you have decided that you would like to work according to a certain schedule, make sure your family knows when, how, and where you will be working. Make sure they know when you will be working and when you won't be. Set ground rules and enlist their help.

Don't Procrastinate

Procrastination is probably the biggest reason why people fail to accomplish their goals and meet their deadlines while maintaining order in their lives. What happens when we procrastinate? We get lazy. We lose momentum. We miss out on opportunities. We are late. We get ourselves in a time crunch. We forfeit peace in our lives and generally get ourselves in a tizzy.

I know all about this from firsthand experience, because I am a "recovering procrastinator." There were those high school days when I would rush in at 9:00 at night and say, "Daddy, you just *have* to type this history paper for me. It's due in the morning and my grade depends on it!" There were those Christmases when I waited until the last minute to shop, and then had to settle for hot pink wool socks for my grandmother.

I'm not talking about situations where you genuinely take on more than you can handle, and as a result get swamped. Nor am I talking about extenuating circumstances which arise and throw a kink in your otherwise-well-laid-out plans. I'm talking about pure and simple procrastination—putting off what you *know* you need to be doing. There will be plenty of situations in a home business like the first two reasons, but procrastination as a reason for problems can and should be dealt with in your life.

If you are a chronic procrastinator, you can overcome this obstacle to peace and success. A slogan from a popular commercial for athletic shoes tells you how: "Just do it." Although the slogan actually refers to exercise, it is also the way to prevent procrastination: *Just do it.* Don't think about it; *do it.* Don't overplan for it; *do it.* Don't just dream about it; *do it.* Proverbs 14:23 says, "In all labor there is profit, but mere talk leads only to poverty." Don't just talk about it. *Do it.*

If you have a project or goal you are trying to accomplish, try this: 1) Write down your goal and action steps to achieve it. 2) On your calendar schedule a start-date, intermittent checkpoints, and a target date for completing whatever it is that you want to do. 3) Check your calendar daily so you can watch your progress. 4) Pray that the Lord will help you overcome your tendency to put things off. If laziness is the reason you put things off, you will have difficulty making your home business a success. At the very least, you will experience frustration. "Laziness casts into a deep sleep, and an idle man will suffer hunger" (Proverbs 19:15). 5) Sometimes it helps to put notes around the house to remind you to begin a project. 6) Do the worst things first. Getting the most unpleasant part out of the way in the beginning can make it easier to finish. 7) Tell your spouse and family or friends that you are working on gaining control over procrastination, and ask for their support and encouragement. Ask them to remind you when they notice you procrastinating and to encourage you when you succeed.

Sometimes people are good at beginning things but poor at completing them. The Bible admonishes us to finish what we start: "But now finish doing it also; that just as there was the readiness to desire it, so there may be also the completion of it by your ability" (2 Corinthians 8:11).

Dedicate Each Day to the Lord

The time you have available each day is given to you by the Lord: "There is an appointed time for everything, and there is a time for every event under heaven" (Ecclesiastes 3:1). Begin your day by dedicating it to the Lord. Ask Him for guidance and for help in using the time He has given you as He sees fit. "In the morning, O Lord, Thou wilt hear my voice; in the morning I will order my prayer to Thee and eagerly watch" (Psalm 5:3). We are accountable to the Lord for how we use our time. Therefore we should make the quality of our time count.

However, this doesn't mean that every moment must be filled with some pressure-filled activity. Rest and times of inactivity are very important. Nor does it mean that our to-do list must always be finished. We should be open to God's interruptions and be ready for whatever God has planned for our day. If things are not going as planned, don't panic. God will bless your day anyway.

We are responsible for what we do with our time *today*, not tomorrow. "Do not boast about tomorrow, for you do not know what a day may bring forth" (Proverbs 27:1). Pray that God will guide you as you strive to use your time to make a difference in things with eternal value.

Time-Management Tips

- Limit outside activities.
  Your time is precious. Make sure you spend your time on the important things.

- Schedule in family time.
  Plan for time to be with your spouse or children. If we don't do this, it's too easy to let the people closest to us get what's left over of our time and energy (if there is any left over), instead of our prime time.

- Plan when you will spend time with the Lord.
  Through prayer and Bible reading, nurture your relationship with your Creator. You need His direction, guidance, and strength to be able to handle the load you have taken on.

- Plan for some free time for yourself.
  Don't leave yourself off the list. You need some R & R time as well.

- Learn to do more than one thing at a time.
  Talk on the phone while you prepare dinner. While you wait in line, make a list of what you must do tomorrow.

- Learn to do things faster.
  Train yourself to make snap decisions over things that really don't matter. Save your time and energy for the important things. Don't dawdle over which kind of pizza to order. Just decide. Don't make a major production over simple things in life. There are plenty of difficult situations that call for more than enough of our time, attention, and energy.

- Use technology to save precious time.
  Take full advantage of microwave ovens, electric brooms, or whatever saves you time. My food processor saves me time, but bugs my husband because it is so loud. When he complained, I just explained that it saved me about eight minutes each time I used it. I use it at least three times a week, so that's almost half an hour a week that I save. Since I'd much rather read a magazine, take a walk, or bake a cake than chop onions or grate cheese, I continue to use it. My husband especially liked the cake idea and is now in favor of the food processor!

- Organize your files to save you time.
  Many types of businesses use "project files." You don't even need to have a business to benefit from organized files for various projects. To save time, write the names, numbers, addresses, and deadlines (as applicable) on the outside of the

folder. Then when you are repeatedly using the material in the folder, you don't have to look elsewhere for that information when you need it—it's all right there in front of you.

• Let your fingers do the walking.
Use your phone book before you make unnecessary trips. Calling ahead can save you not only time and money but frustration as well.

• Keep a pen and paper by your bed, in your car, and in your briefcase or purse at all times.
You never know when the inspiration will hit! There have been many times when I have solved a problem or come up with a great idea while trying to go to sleep. That's also the time when I occasionally remember something to do the next day that I hadn't written on my list. If you don't write it down when you think of it, you may lose the thought.

• Take breaks.
This can give you the necessary mental and physical renewal you need to get going again.

• Work smarter, not harder.
Use mind over muscle to save you time. Think things through before beginning to see if there is any way to save time.

• Don't travel in rush hour.

• Put idle time to work for you.
Use in-between time to your advantage. Carry a small book, or an article you want to read with you. Read that article while

you stand in line. Make out your grocery list while you are waiting at the dentist. Empty the trash during the commercials of a program you are watching or listening to. There are countless things that can be done during the small snatches of time between the activities of your day.

• Strive to simplify your life.
  The more you can simplify your life, the easier it will be to manage your time.

There will be days when your time-management system is just not working and you feel like you're about to lose it. When time problems get the best of you and the home business path gets a little rocky, don't stop at just counting to ten or taking a hot bubble bath. Try these five-minute breaks:

1. Quote a Scripture. Examples: "I can do all things through Christ, who strengthens me"; "Do your work as unto the Lord"; "Greater is He who is in you than he who is in the world."

2. Pray.

3. Make a mental note of a blessing from the Lord that day.

4. Tell someone that blessing. Be a testimony!

5. Hug your spouse.

6. Hug your kids.

7. Listen to Christian music.

8. Sing a praise song.

9. Read a psalm.

10. Think of three reasons why you feel the Lord has blessed you with a home business.

10
Managing Your Home

To some it may sound like Utopia—to run your own business from the comfort of your own home with your spouse and/or little darlings all around you. But the little darlings are not always little angels, and family life and business paraphernalia do not exactly produce tidy homes. The supermom (or superdad) syndrome is much easier to fall into while working at home. In fact it takes real effort to avoid trying to become one. It also takes effort to keep from feeling guilty because you can't seem to become a superperson.

But don't worry—with the 80's behind us, hopefully so is the decade of the superperson ideal. I think women in particular are tired of feeling as if they have to reach for the brass ring and "be all that they could be" while simultaneously looking great, feeling great, and running a great home. Add a home business to that picture and you're sure to come up with an unwieldy situation. If you have ever struggled with trying to "keep it all together," you are joined by millions of others. Take solace in the fact that you actually *can* have it all; you just can't have it all *at the same time*.

Your most obvious question right now is how you can manage a business at home when managing your children and your household took all your time before. Running a successful home often requires you to be a babysitter, maid, and cook, in addition to being a CEO, administrator, and social director. So how do you continue to have a well-managed home and also a home business? Know that you cannot do everything yourself! Reevaluate how you run your home, decide what can be eliminated, get extra help, set aside time to maintain your home, readjust your standards, and organize your home.

Reevaluate How You Run Your Home

Begin by finding a quiet place, and seek out the Lord to give you wisdom and guidance as you plan. Then *write down* everything you can possibly think of that you do during the course of a week, and when you do it. Write down anything additional that comes up during the month that requires your time. Then further divide that into daily activities. You may be amazed that you have any energy left over after looking at your list! Next, on a separate piece of paper write down what you consider priorities in your life—things like time to play with your kids, time alone with your husband, your quiet time with the Lord, time for exercise, and so forth. Now go back to your activity list and put a checkmark in the margin next to all the activities that are also on your priority list. The more checkmarks you have, the better you are doing at balancing your life and doing what is important. If you don't have as many checks as you'd like, don't worry; you are now taking action to spend time on the things you value as priorities.

Decide What Can Be Eliminated

Now take a good long look at that activity list and mark through anything that can be cut out. At first glance it may seem that nothing can be crossed off, but the more you consider your list, the more you may find that you can eliminate some of your activities. If you try to run your home as you did before and accomplish everything on your list in addition to running your business, you will run yourself into an early grave. Remember, don't try to be a superwoman. You may love a class at the community college you take, a hobby, a Bible study, or a club you belong to, but something has to give. There may be time in your life later for these activities. If you are combining your home business with being the primary manager of your household, and especially if children are in the picture, some of the things in your life may need to be put on hold. The point is to simplify your life as much as possible so that you don't go crazy trying to run your home and your home business.

Get Extra Help

And now to the fun part of the list process: Give some of your work to others! When I asked a friend how he managed everything in his life, Larry said he did three things: "Delegate. Delegate. Delegate." A good rule of thumb!

Mark all the things on the list that can be delegated. *You* don't have to do all the laundry. *You* don't have to cook all the meals all the time. Someone else can take out the garbage, and so forth. You may find you need help in your business, in your home, or with your children.

You can have your children do some of the tasks. And your husband can become your helpmate in the truest sense of the word. Having a home business will mean teamwork, so be frank in the beginning and go over the list with your family, letting them decide which things they would like to do. Some people have even had their spouses join them full-time in their home business, which really lightens the load.

Since one of the goals of having a business is to provide an income, use some of that money to hire someone to help you. Consider it a necessary expense for your business (not to mention you). Dr. James Dobson has said that the fatigue-and-time-pressure syndrome is one of the top causes of depression among women. Many families have prioritized things they would like when they have enough money, but Dr. Dobson says, "It is my conviction that domestic help for the mother of small children should appear on that priority list too. Without it, she is sentenced to the same responsibilities day in and day out, seven days a week. It is my belief that she will do a more efficient job in those tasks and be a better mother if she can share the load with someone else occasionally."[1] That is especially true of the woman who is a homemaker *and* has a home business. You essentially have two jobs, and you will function better in both jobs if you do not bear the workload alone.

You do not have to pay for an expensive maid service if you need help in cleaning the house. Teenagers or college students are often more than willing to earn some money by helping you out. A friend of mine hires a teenager in her neighborhood to do a varied assortment of odd jobs at her home, such as cleaning, ironing, cooking a meal once or twice a week, and anything she can think of to free up more of her time for the things which she cannot delegate. Another friend makes good use of the teenage babysitters she hires in the evenings, who would otherwise be watching TV for several hours after the kids are in bed. When she hires them, she asks if they want the $3.00 plan or the $4.00 plan. With the $4.00 plan she leaves a list of simple things to do after the children are in bed, such as washing the dishes, folding laundry, or dusting.

Put a note on the bulletin board at your church describing the kind of help you need. Call other area churches and ask if they know of people looking for work. Run an ad in your community paper. Tell your friends that you want to hire some help. Call a local high school counselor and ask for recommendations of responsible students to help with some cleaning. Or you can use a maid service. This is usually pretty expensive, but it might be worth it if you just need occasional help and you don't have any other means of getting it. As Luanne Shackelford has said, "It's cheaper than room and board in the funny farm."[2]

Some of my clients and friends used to accuse me of being supermom as I tried to run my business, keep my children at home, home-school my kindergartner, freelance in the news reporting business, write, and so on. I must confess—I am not this all-together wonder-woman; I simply have outside help! In the beginning I tried to do everything myself. Things would go okay for awhile, but then the work would begin to accumulate, as would the laundry and the dishes. Sometimes it looked like World War Three had broken out in our house. I knew I would probably have more time with my children, my husband, and my house if I just got a "normal" job, but I was dedicated to working at home. One day had been particularly bad. It was 1:00 in the morning and I was working on a deadline. My kids had vegged out in front of the TV, there were toys everywhere, no one had clean clothes, the bathrooms were a mess, and we had ordered dinner out (again). I was feeling extremely tired and horribly guilty.

After I had a good cry, a talk with the Lord, and a brainstorming session with my husband, we decided to get some help. We now have someone who comes into our home on a regular, part-time basis to help with the children and the house. Ida has been a blessing in our home and the only way I am able to run my business when it gets busy without sacrificing my family. Now instead of finishing my business work only to start my housework, I am able to spend more time with my family, which is the whole reason I want to work at home in the first place.

A friend once asked me if I ever missed cleaning my own house. While I never really get a strong urge to scrub the toilets, I do enjoy taking care of my family and my home. I count it a joy to be able to see to the needs of my children, to make home a nice place to be, and to be a helpmate to my husband. But I also have to be realistic. I could not continue to do this full-time and run a business at the same time without some assistance. There are periods of time when my helper doesn't come and I juggle my business with my household responsibilities. (The kids accompany me on client deliveries, my 5-year-old "helps" me clean the house, and my husband mops the floor.) When my housekeeper resumes her schedule with me, the load is much lighter.

One thing that has worked well for me is to share outside help with other people. Regular part-time help can be difficult to find. Several of my friends also needed occasional help with their homes or children, so we all share Ida's time. She likes it because she is working full-time, and it works out great for us too. One added advantage is that since everyone that she works for is acquainted, we can be flexible in when she works.

Set Aside Time to Maintain Your Home

Now that you know what you need to do on a routine basis to keep your household going, and what you need help with, decide when you will do it. If you just wait until the mood hits you to do the shopping or scrub the tub, you could be waiting a long time, especially when your business gets busy. Some people like to set aside particular days for particular household maintenance chores (vacuuming on Monday, wash on Tuesday, etc.). Others like to set aside a certain time of each day to do these things ("I'll clean for an hour each morning before I begin working" or "I'll do the shopping in the evenings"). Others like to set aside one day that is devoted strictly to household duties. This is particularly common for people working at home on a part-time basis. That is how Barbara keeps her home managed. "I reserve Monday for 'home day.' We don't plan any activities that day. We go to the grocery store, run all our errands, clean the house, plan the menu for the week, and do the laundry. If something comes up that I really want to do on Monday, I'll take out time the weekend before because my "home work" really has to be done by Monday night. There is still straightening throughout the week, but if I plan well, most of the work can be done on Monday. I really can't be free of the house if I'm stringing out the work all week." Things will come up which will prevent you from sticking to your plan occasionally, and many people purposely deviate from their schedule to escape routine. That's fine, but at least creating some kind of plan to accomplish home maintenance is better than a shot-in-the-dark approach, hoping you will find the time to fit it all in. Sarah is a good example. "Home is a real priority with me because I really get stressed if it's not organized. You can't do things as they come up like 'Oh, we've run out of clean clothes. We need to wash clothes.' You have to work ahead and be organized. Even though I stress being organized, I'm not a routine person to do certain things on certain days. I do look ahead, though, especially when I'm busy with work, to make time to do things that are needed."

Readjust Your Standards

Back to the question of how to get everything done that you did before you had your home business. After you eradicate the nonessential things in your life, garner the support and assistance from your family, and hire out some of the tasks that you can delegate, there is another step: *You may need to readjust your standards in certain areas of your life.* "Lower my standards? Never!" you may say. But in the long run you will find that you do indeed need to *adjust* if not lower your standards in the things that don't really matter. Who cares if your sheets have hospital corners on all the beds in your house? Does it really matter that every can in your pantry is stacked alphabetically, and all your clothing hangs in your closet according to color? What *does* count is that your bed is made, there is food in the pantry, and you have clean clothes in your closet. Decide which areas of your life you will feel comfortable adjusting in order to create more time for your business. Don't lower your standards on the things that are important to you or your family. But evaluate what really matters and what doesn't. Don't take time away from the things that are important (your relationship with the Lord, your family, your business) to do things that are not a priority.

Organize Your Home

If your home lacks organization, now is the best time to get organized. You will need your home functioning at its best in order to be able to run a business at the same time. Clean out closets, discover what's under your bed, and be able to locate your personal files quickly. Organize your wardrobe, your kitchen, your cleaning supplies, and your storage system. If you don't have a storage system, try Emilie Barnes' "Total Mess to Total Rest" plan that she details in her books *More Hours in My Day* and *Survival for Busy Women*. Go through your house with a number of large plastic bags and organize your possessions. For each item, either put it away, throw it away, or store it. Store your things in numbered boxes. Make out a three-by-five card listing what you have stored and in which box you put it. Keep these alphabetically listed in a card file. Then you can find whatever you need in seconds. For a more detailed look at organizing your home from stem to stern, read Emilie's books. You will never think the same way about household organization again! After you get everything organized, don't forget to maintain it regularly. This will be your key to an efficiently run home. Besides, who wants to go through the total mess part again? Also, keep the quantity of your things pared down. It's easier to be organized if you just have fewer things to organize.

Another way to stay organized and ahead of the game is to do as much as possible prior to when you need it. If you have a morning meeting, lay out your briefcase, papers, or other materials the night before. Also lay out your children's clothes, school things, and lunches the night before.

Take advantage of sales, and avoid a last-minute dash to the store for gifts or cards. Set aside a gift shelf with gifts that you can grab in a moment's notice for that occasion you forgot, or just to save time. Make a list of cards you want to give throughout the year, and buy them at one time. Write down these occasions on your calendar. When the birthday rolls around, you won't be making a special trip to the store.

Plan your menus and your grocery list at the same time. Plan for at least a week at a time to avoid impulse purchases and to cut down on trips. I used to go to the store a couple of times a week until I started making out my menus for a month at a time. Now I make my grocery list from that menu and shop at a wholesale club where I can buy in bulk. Not only do I save money, but I don't run out of things as quickly. What I can't use right away, I freeze. Then I only have to make a quick trip to the local grocery store once a week for fresh foods. I plan a certain number of meals for the month and pick which meal I feel like having on the day I am going to prepare it. (Relegating particular meals for particular days is a bit too regimented for me.) This frees me not only from running out of things and overspending, but also from standing over my cookbooks wondering what I can fix for dinner.

When possible, try to prepare your meals in advance. One busy home-business owner begins as much of her dinner as possible while in the kitchen for breakfast or lunch. If you have a large enough freezer, fix your meals in advance and freeze them. Make double recipes and freeze one meal. Some people like to pick one day a week where they will do several days' worth of cooking. There have been plenty of evenings when I was grateful, after a hectic day, to have a nice meal ready in minutes thanks to my preparation, my freezer, and my microwave!

11

Where Do the Children Fit In?

The room had that "well-lived-in" look. Artboards from my current desktop publishing jobs were lying on the bed in various stages of completion. My latest writing project was in front of me as I struggled to edit with one hand and nurse the baby with the other. My five-year-old was singing as she colored on the floor beside me. My two-year-old was blissfully playing in a sinkful of bubbles in the bathroom next to me. From where I was sitting I could see all of this, and I suddenly realized, "So *this* is how working at home with children can be!" They were looking rather angelic, I was getting something done, and we were all quite happy. I wish I could tell you it's always that much fun or always that easy, but I have to be truthful: Working at home with children, especially young children, is very, well, let's just say . . . character-building! It can also be fun, rewarding, crazy, loud, silly, trying, and irreplaceable. I wouldn't want to miss a minute of it!

One of the nicest places a mother can be is at home with her children, especially in the early years, and more mothers than you may think feel this same way. Many would have you believe that this country is suffering from a daycare crisis, since the mothers of more than half the 9 million U.S. children under age three have or are looking for outside jobs.[1] Some reports tell us that over half of all women in this country with kids under six are working, but only 29 percent of them are doing so full-time.[2]

Some researchers estimate that about half of all home-workers are women, and that about 6 million are self-employed women. Some reports say that well over 1 million American women work an average of 27 hours a week for pay at home, and that nearly 600,000 of those women have a child under the age of six at home.[3]

The real truth is that while there are vast numbers of women entering the workforce, the traditional family is not dead, and many mothers desire to be home with their children.

A 1987 Census Bureau report titled *Who's Minding the Kids?* showed that half of all preschool children are still being cared for by Mom at home. About 75 percent are being cared for by some relative, whether Mom, Grandma, or Aunt Mary. This means that only 25 percent of preschool children are being cared for by a non-relative full-time.[4] That's radically different from what we're hearing about the shortage of daycare centers.

What's more, many of those women in the workforce don't really want to be there. "Focus on the Family" reported that 68 percent of those surveyed said they thought it was important for families to make financial sacrifices so that one parent could be home with the children. Only 27 percent said they thought financial gains were more important.[5] Several major polls have shown that a majority of women would rather be home when they have small children. One of them revealed that 80 percent of American women who are in the workforce and who are mothers would rather be at home if economically they could afford to do so. Another public-opinion poll done in 1988 showed that 88 percent of mothers with children under age 18 agreed with the statement "If I could afford it, I would rather be at home with my children."[6]

Another study on this issue was done by the Mark Clemens Research Corporation, commissioned by *Glamour* magazine. Women were asked to agree or disagree with this statement: "If I could afford to do so, I would prefer to be at home raising my children rather than earning income outside the home." The research group only surveyed mothers already working. It did not include women who were already at home, which would obviously have skewed the results. About 84 percent said they would rather be at home![7]

Besides the fact that so many mothers want to be home with their children, daycare just isn't that great for our kids. The Heritage Foundation put out a report that was widely publicized. Bill Mattox, with the Family Research Council, describes that report: "It showed that a lot of the most recent data on substitute care arrangements for children disclosed that children who spend a fair amount of time in some type of daycare setting tend to have some negative experiences. This is not an iron rule, but general trends show that kids in those situations often tend to be less attached to their parents, more likely to be engaged in various types of aggression, and often have difficulty in school." That is no news to many of the moms whose children are in daycare. Add to that the difficulty when your children are ill and can't go to the center, when your child cries when you leave, when your child comes home sick from the latest outbreak at the daycare center, and the list goes on.

Sharon is one of the many mothers who does not want her child in daycare. "I want to be able to watch my son grow. In daycare there are so many illnesses, and you don't really know what's going on during the day. By working at home, now I do know, and we're closer than any other situation could allow." Since so many mothers want to be with their children, and so many children want and need to be with their mothers, working at home is becoming a popular solution.

So How Do You Work at Home with Children?

It is possible to work at home with children and retain the right to be their primary caregiver, but how do you go about it? How do you really run a business with little ones around? Some people will tell you it cannot be done successfully, at least with any degree of professionalism. Others may tell you it's a breeze. I'll tell you that both are wrong, but that with dedication and the Lord's wisdom you can do it. You just have to be creative and have a lot of patience, endless energy, and a good supply of crayons!

How can you combine the two jobs? One home-worker said, "I cannot put in a full eight-hour day. I have to divide myself between him and work, and that's one of the drawbacks of working at home. I can't give 100 percent to work and 100 percent to my child during the day. But I feel that being with him during the day, with him able to interact with me, is worth dividing myself. I don't have the daycare worries at all, which is worth a lot." Heidi says, "It's a matter of juggling priorities every day. My main priority is to be a good mother for my little girl at home. Sometimes an immediate deadline for a project will take precedence over time that I can spend with her, but I try to juggle things so that I'm not away from her on a full-time basis."

Juggling priorities and sharing time between two jobs is a major part of the solution, but there will be times when your children may have to be in substitute care in order for you to do your job. This type of situation is different from the typical daycare scenario, since that's one of the reasons you are working at home in the first place. Daycare centers don't even have to be on your option list. Barbara sums it up well: "You have to be flexible. You can't say 'I'm never going to be away from my child. I'm never going to have any type of daycare.' I think people who do that aren't allowing for any adjustments in their lives. I think you have to go into your business with the attitude, 'What does the Lord want me to do right now?' "

Home-schooling mother and author Luanne Shackelford has said, "We may never get written up in *Redbook* as Wondermom of the Year, but hopefully we will make it through one day, and then another, and then another, and so on until we are old ladies. Then our kids will come back to us and say, 'Mom, I don't know how you ever did it!' and we can look very wise and say, 'Hmm... I did it one day at a time, that's how.' "[8] These words were written in reference to home-schooling, but you too are attempting to do two things simultaneously: Run your business and raise your children. The best way to approach that feat is definitely one day at a time.

One Scripture that has carried me through time and time again is Psalm 68:19: "Blessed be the Lord, who daily bears our burden, the God who is our salvation." Working at home with small children is particularly tough, but God has promised that if He is our Lord and Savior, He will carry us through on a day-to-day basis. And He has done so for me many, many times.

So what are the options when you need help in supervising the children?

1. *Share responsibility with your spouse.* Take turns, juggle shifts, and share the load to enable you to work while your mate watches the children. This works well for women who work part-time, and it helps if your spouse has a somewhat flexible schedule. Many couples have gone into business full-time together at home. This is a great option for the children. They get to be influenced by both of their parents, and Mom and Dad can share the workload. Work out an arrangement with your mate for some time off from the kids so you can work in your business.

2. *Pay older siblings to babysit the younger ones.* If you have several children, occasionally hire the oldest to corral the young ones. They can take the little ones to the park, go for walks, play in the backyard with them, and supervise them in arts and crafts. The older ones will enjoy earning some money while at the same time learning responsibility. Just be careful of giving older kids *too* much responsibility. They are still children themselves. If you need regular care, consider other options, since children need to be raised by adults, not older children.

3. *Barter babysitting time with a friend.* Find someone whom you trust, and exchange childcare services with her. This is a great option if you can find someone who is available when you need her, who shares your views about what's allowed, and who will reciprocate the time. The best part of this plan is that neither of you is out any money. Some people like this idea because it gives them an opportunity to work undisturbed without the children in the house. If the other family has children who are close in age to yours, they both get new playmates.

4. *Hire outside help.* This is a tough issue because many people are stuggling just to be able to give working at home a try, and cannot even consider paying for help. Even if you take working at home out of the picture, it is important to keep expenses down in the start-up phase of most new businesses. However, if you cannot garner help in other ways, sometimes it becomes imperative to hire part-time help with the children in order to enable you to do your work, call on clients, deliver goods, etc. For many people, one of the nice things about working at home is that even if you find that you *do* have to hire help, you have the option of having your children cared for in your home, where you still get to be near them. Traditional employees do not usually have the option of

bringing the kids to work. Another plus is that you get to determine if and when you need childcare help, and for how long.

Even though parental care is best for children, there may come a time when you just need some help to keep your business going. It is for this reason that I mention various options. Childcare assistance can come in the form of a relative, a neighborhood family daycare setting, a preschool, a mother's-day-out program, and in-home care providers.

- *A relative.* If you are blessed enough to live in the same area as your relative, consider hiring your mother, your grandmother, your sister, or someone else in the family to help you with the children. The children benefit from establishing a closer relationship with the relative than they otherwise might, and you will know your child's caregiver pretty well. Extended families used to be closer, with Grandma often living down the street, but society today tends to be spread all over the globe. If you are blessed to live close to a relative with whom you would feel comfortable watching your children, and if he or she wants to do it, this is an ideal option for many home-workers.

- *A neighborhood family daycare setting.* This is a place where mothers stay home to care for their children, and will care for yours too in their homes. These are not "daycare centers" like the structured programs we talked about before, but care in a family/home situation. Some homes take only full-time children, but many will take part-timers and drop-ins. I used this type of childcare when I worked at an "outside" job, and the woman I found was a dream. My daughter loved to go to her house and became very close to her children, even celebrating birthdays together. We shared the same values and she prayed for my daughter. The local kiddie-corral franchise down the street certainly wouldn't provide this type of care.

• *A church-sponsored mother's-day-out or preschool.* Many local churches are providing drop-in mother's-day-out services where you can take your child for about five hours a day at a very reasonable fee. The best part of this care is that your children are allowed to be taught spiritual values in most of these church programs, unlike the secular centers. You can usually leave your child one or two days a week for mother's-day-out programs and two to three days for preschool programs. Preschools are usually for older preschool children and provide more of a structured learning experience. Some churches even have a drop-in program as frequently as six days a week. One woman who uses a mother's-day-out program a few hours a week takes her child to the church 30 minutes earlier than usual before a business meeting. Then she goes back home to finish getting ready, gather her things, and leave with a peaceful heart instead of being totally stressed out. Her child also gets more of her attention during the morning, as well as a more relaxed mom.

• *An in-home care provider.* Hiring someone to come into your home to care for your children is not just a choice for the rich. There are two options: live-out and live-in.

Live-out help might be a teenager, a neighbor, a college student, or an elderly person who needs part-time work. It might be your mother. It could be a childcare-provider/ housekeeper who works for you and others on a part-time basis. Or it could be a trained nanny. The cost can range from $2.00 an hour for a teenager to $200 a week (and up) for a nanny. The options are as varied as the needs that people have. (You may find that your needs change from time to time as well.)

Several ways to find household help were mentioned in the last chapter. They can also be a means to find childcare help. Ask your friends if they know of anyone looking for work. Perhaps their helper might want to work for you too, or they may know of someone else who would. Put an ad on your church bulletin board. Call local churches to see if they know of someone looking for this type of work. Ask your friends or the youth director at your church for reliable sitters.

One home-based worker has found that occasional after-school help is all she needs. "I pay a teenager $2.00 an hour to come in after school several days a week to play with my child and do odd jobs for me. My child looks forward to when she comes over, and it frees up time for me to work undisturbed."

Going through a nanny service may be the quickest way to find someone (and the service screens the applicants before you interview them), but this is also the costliest way to go. The one-time fee which the services charge to find you a nanny can run from $500 to $1200 or more for a full-time person. Then the weekly cost of the nanny in most urban areas starts at $200 a week.

Live-in help can be cheaper than full-time live-out help, since you are providing room and board. Costs will vary, depending on whether the person speaks English and where you live. It costs an average of about $45 in my area to have a maid service come for a light cleaning. She is usually only in your home for half a day. For about what it would cost you to have the maid come three half-days, you could usually find a foreign-speaking live-in who would be there full-time. Another live-in source is through an au pair program. This is where you provide room, board, and a paid vacation for a foreign girl, usually 18-25 years old. The weekly salary range is $100-160, depending on the program, and sometimes you pay the airfare here for the girl as well. She usually stays with the family for one year. Check your phone book for au pair programs available in your area.

Please don't think that by "live-in help" I mean maids wearing little uniforms and serving rich, lazy folks. That is not what I mean. For some people in some situations a live-in might be what they need, particularly if they have a large family or other special needs. Having a full-time person in your home does not mean relegating all authority to the "nursemaid," letting someone else raise your kids. It just means that you need help. You do have to be *extremely* careful when you bring someone into your home, since she will have great influence on your family. You also need to consider whether you have the room, and how much privacy your family needs. Some people are very much against this type of help, while others long for it. I am not advocating it, nor do I want to breed discontent in your heart; I just want to present it as an option.

Most home-workers do not need this much help. If all the help you have is from your husband a few hours in the evenings and on a Saturday morning now and then, be grateful that you have a husband who is willing to do that much. Pray that the person you hire will not only be good for your family, but that your family will be a blessing to her as well. No matter how much help you have (or don't have) in running your home, caring for your children, or running your business, thank the Lord for the blessings He has provided.

Since one of the main reasons many people work at home is to be with their children more, there will be many times when you will be working with them around. If you have preschoolers at home, the picture really gets complicated. Where *do* the children fit in? These ideas are not meant to take the place of supervised childcare for extended periods of time while you are working, since young children need constant supervision. However, these ideas may help keep your children occupied long enough for you to finish that project or make a few business calls.

Tips for Working with Young Children Around

1. *Work when they are sleeping.* This is a favorite! You get more done and you *know* they are safe! Try getting up earlier and/or staying up later and working during nap

times to get as much done as possible when they are asleep. Stacey combines this with other help as well. "I have my children in mother's-day-out two days a week (a total of ten hours), and probably get in another hour-and-a-half a day between naps and after bedtime or when they are watching TV, plus another five hours when I have a sitter at the house. I'm probably getting in between 20 and 30 hours a week with my business. There are still plenty of days of McDonald's Happy Meals and afternoons at the park, but on those days I'm usually making phone calls in the morning while they watch 'Sesame Street,' and doing paperwork at the desk while they nap."

2. *Provide special toys to play with when you are working.* Set aside a box with toys that they can use only during your worktime. Make these "special" toys, and change what's in the box frequently. Put surprises in the box from time to time for them to find.

3. *Give them their own "work area" near yours.* Set aside a small area near where you work so they can "work" alongside you. Give them a box or a tray with their own special supplies to be used only during your working hours. Let them have their own envelopes, paper, scissors, crayons, paperclips, tapes, and other office supplies so they can occupy themselves while in your sight. My daughter loves this and has made hundreds of special creations while we both work.

4. *Fill a sink or plastic tub with sudsy water and lots of Tupperware.* Small children love to wash dishes. If you work close enough to a sink that you can see or hear them, let them wash all the plastic dishes you can find. If not, lay several towels under a plastic tub for dishwashing fun. This can keep some children busy for almost an

hour. Sometimes a few puddles are worth 45 minutes to finish a project.

5. *Set your children up at a table near you with special activities.* Let them do puzzles. Make paperclip necklaces, paper chains, macaroni art, etc. Get out the shaving cream and plastic aprons or big T-shirts, and let them smear it all over the table. They love this!

6. *Save all your junk mail for them.*

7. *Rotate their toys.* Don't keep all your children's toys out at the same time. Put some of them in boxes or large trash bags and store them. Then once a month or so, bring out the "new" toys and put away some of the ones they have been playing with. This helps keep your children from getting bored with their things.

8. *Keep a cabinet or drawer just for your children.* Fill it with old pots and pans, plastic dishes, or junk odds and ends that you don't mind them playing with. Little ones especially will think they are really into things, which is often half their fun.

9. *Get a special videotape that they can watch only when you work.* If you have a VCR, you can rent videos, or else buy one and bring it out only occasionally to keep it "special." Many videos are educational and entertaining, and many excellent Christian videos are available as well. To save money, tape PBS specials, Christmas specials, and other good family viewing. If you have opted to get rid of your television, you can buy special videotape monitors that do not receive TV signals. This way you can control what your family watches.

10. *Use monitored TV.* I'm not talking about plunking your kids in front of the tube for an afternoon of Teenage

Mutant Ninja Turtles and Ghostbusters. TV can be harmful to children, which is why it is *so* important to monitor what they watch and to limit the time they are allowed to watch it. What good does it do to work at home if the little ones are glued to the boob tube for hours on end? However, many people have found that an occasional viewing of "Sesame Street" or "Mr. Rogers' Neighborhood" isn't so terrible. But be warned: "Good" TV is often linked with bad commercials! If you can't be in the room when your children are watching TV, stick to PBS or videotapes. Just don't get dependent on the TV to babysit the kids; it's easy to do when you work at home, but costly for your children.

11. *Buy a two-gallon cooler with a pushbutton and paper cups.* Keep this in the kitchen within reach so the kids can help themselves. This can save you hundreds of trips to the kitchen!

Other Ways to Work at Home with Children

1. *Set ground rules.* It is important to establish a set of rules that will work for you and your family. Make it clear to your children what you expect, what is allowed, and what is not allowed while you are working. If you have business hours, make sure your children know this. Let them know what things they may touch and which areas are hands-off. Are they allowed to answer the phone? (This is not a good idea if your business line is also your home number, and clients will be calling.) Can they answer only during certain times? Tell your children what you expect of them when you are on a business call. If you don't tell them, most children will still ask you for a drink and cry for justice when sister takes their favorite toy no matter if you are on the phone to the President! (Incidentally, phone silencers are made that cut out background noise when the other party is talking.) Are they

allowed to interrupt your work whenever they want to, or do you have "Do Not Disturb" times? I have tried to establish an open/shut door policy. "When Mommy's office door is shut, that means I'm working. If my door is open, that means you may come in and I will be happy to talk with you. Unless someone is bleeding or the house is on fire, please ask Daddy instead of knocking on my door." This is a hard rule to implement, and it obviously only works if another adult is in the house, or your children are older. The five-year-old is beginning to get this, but the two-year-old needs a lot of reminding!

Karen has been pretty successful in teaching her son when she can be disturbed and when she can't. She taught him that it was important not to interrupt her while she is in the middle of sewing an appliqué piece, but if she comes to a pivot point on the garment where she has to stop and turn the fabric, it's okay to talk. Jerasen has learned by the sound of the machine and by looking at where the needle is on the garment when she is about to stop. He waits until she reaches that point to talk with her, so she doesn't make any mistakes or have to ask him to be quiet. Now that's cooperation! If you expect your children to obey your rules while you are working, make certain that they know what the rules are in advance, and be consistent in implementing them.

2. *Include them in your work when you can.* Including your children in your work when possible makes your children feel more a part of your life. When Daddy goes off to the office day after day, how many children really understand what it is that Daddy does? When Daddy works at home, the children can better understand how Daddy spends his time, especially if he makes an effort to include his children whenever possible. Let them stuff envelopes, help box products, or accompany you on business errands or deliveries. Depending on the nature of your business and the ages of your children, there are

many ways to involve your kids in your work. One mother who has a baking business said, "My children now know what it takes to get food on the table. They see that baked goods don't just come from the grocery store. They've helped me make the things I sell and have seen the process needed to get them there." Your children can learn skills and the value of hard work. They can learn responsibility while nurturing family bonds. You will have the opportunity to teach and influence them not only in what you are doing but also in the way you work and the attitude you have about your work. If your children see you "working as unto the Lord," they will have someone to emulate. Involving our children can produce spiritual growth in their lives as well as our own.

3. *Schedule breaks with your children.* Stop working periodically to spend some time with your children. If they are at home while you are working, stop for a few minutes. Read a story. Build a Lego building. Color a picture. Play with paper dolls. It may take only 15 minutes, but the break will do both you and your child good. Besides, how many nine-to-fivers do you know who can fingerpaint in the middle of the day? If your children are being cared for away from your home, plan on a break when you can be together so they can have your undivided attention. And don't refuse to allow unplanned breaks. Sometimes your children really need you *now*, not in 30 minutes. If your child keeps interrupting you, stop. Maybe all he really wants is a hug and 60 seconds in your lap before he's off to play again.

4. *Implement a "kids' time."* Set aside a special time of the day for your children that is just for them. Maybe midmorning is craft time. Perhaps just before naptime is story hour. Maybe you have a special snack and a listening ear when your kids come home from school. When your children know that you make time for them, in

addition to your business, they will be less likely to resent the time you spend working. Even if you work full-time at home, you can make this a habit that you and your children can come to love. Sometimes when my girls and I are engrossed in something together during our special time and the phone rings, my daughter will say, "Mommy, please just let the machine get it!" And I do. There will be times when certain deadlines may prevent you from having this extended one-on-one time with them, but that can be the exception instead of the norm. If you work only part-time, then time with the children probably isn't a problem. Full-time work at home and a growing business can sometimes make it difficult to spend the quality and quantity of time desirable with our children if we are not careful, especially since we cannot leave our work to "go home."

5. *Plan a special activity or outing.* Plan something special to do with your children (or as a family) each week or month, or whatever suits your family. Mark it on the calendar so your children can see when this will happen. Go skating. Take a walk. Have a picnic. Go to a museum. Do something fun with your kids and involve them in the decision of what you will do. You might even let this be a special reward for following your "work-at-home rules."

6. *Let your children know when you will be finished working.* Time is a difficult thing for young children to grasp, and not knowing when you will be done working is frustrating for kids. They always seem to want you *now*. When they ask when you will be finished, don't say, "Soon" or "Later." Give them a time and honor your word. If your children are too young to tell time, set a timer and tell them you'll be done when the bell rings. Or say, "When this big hand is on the 12" or "When Mr. Rogers is over" or "When the numbers on the clock say

three zero zero." Perhaps if they know when you will be finished, they won't keep coming in every five minutes to ask if you're done yet.

7. *Pray for your children often.* Pray for their safety and protection while you work. Pray that they will learn and grow from your business experience, and that it will be a positive influence in their lives. Pray that the children will see God working in your life and in your business, and that they will grow spiritually.

Fitting children into a work-at-home routine is certainly not the easy path to take; it is a challenge. It takes creativity, forethought, and effort to be able to work at home when you have children. It also takes a sense of humor. My two-year-old is quite attached to her "blankie," but if it doesn't happen to be available, anything silky will suffice. Consequently, I have thought of getting a padlock for my lingerie drawer! My husband and I were desperately trying to get her to break this habit. One day I was in the back of the house when the doorbell rang. I opened the door and a client of mine stepped into the entryway. Out of the corner of my eye and directly behind him I saw my formerly neat den with the contents of that lingerie drawer strewn all over the floor. I quickly escorted my unsuspecting guest into the kitchen, asked him to please have a seat, and fast and furiously gathered my belongings. After he left I tried to explain to my little one that what she had done was a no-no. A short while later I had to drop some work off at another client's office. I did my business and left the office, but as I was walking across the parking lot toward my car, I looked down and saw a remnant from that lingerie escapade sticking telltale out of my boot. (Guess who had been playing at my feet!) My red face and I drove away . . . quickly.

Even though you sometimes have to struggle to maintain a level of professionalism and use all the ingenuity you have to make working at home with kids possible, it is still fun. And it is worth it. At times when my children have to be in the care of someone other than myself for any length of time, one thing is brought to mind dramatically—how much I would miss them if that were the norm. My heart bleeds for the vast number of women who want to be home with their children but can't because of outside jobs.

My third child was born during labor—the labor over this book. While I was finishing it up, I naturally took him with me everywhere I went, as nursing mothers so often do! It was great to be able to stop my writing or interviews and nurse my baby. I loved being able to give my keyboard a break and help my eight-week-old baby practice his smiles and coos. I was reminded of friends who told me that they had to go back to work when their babies were six weeks old. I looked at my son and thanked my heavenly Father that He has given me a home business. I also prayed for the women who are struggling with the decision to make the same step.

If you have very young children or a big family, remember that your load is heavier than most, but you don't have to go it alone. If you feel that the Lord is leading you toward working at home, remember that He promises to bear your burdens daily. Psalm 113:9 says, "He makes the barren woman abide in the house as a joyful mother of children. Praise the Lord!" Not only is this talking about answered prayer for the childless, but the woman in that verse did most of her abiding at home with her children around, and she was *happy* about it!

Don't dwell on how long it will be before your baby is in school so you can really get some work done, or how much easier it is for so-and-so, whose older children don't require constant supervision. The time we have with our children goes by all too quickly. We are accountable for what we do with that time to make a difference for eternity in our children. Jean Fleming said in her book *A Mother's Heart*, "I have no regrets about the years I have spent as a full-time wife and mother. The aspect of mothering that excites me most is the knowledge that I am making a permanent difference in my children's lives." I pray that, like Mrs. Fleming, I too will be able to look back in years to come and say that I have no regrets. Working at home is a way to make that difference while bringing in an income, without just depending on "quality time" before and after an outside job.

If you're wondering whether you will be able to work with your kids around, just take a big breath, pray for patience and inspiration, and accept the challenge with joy. It's worth it!

12

Telecommuting and Working for Others

Starting your own business is certainly not the only way to be home-based. Combining traditional job security and a regular paycheck with home-based employment activity is just what many people are looking for. Telecommuting is simply working at home for someone else using electronic equipment (usually computers) to communicate. Many people love the idea of telecommuting because it gives them an opportunity to forgo the traffic and to work at home without the risk of a business start-up. They can stay on the company payroll and be at home at the same time. One telecommuter said, "At home my office is large, I have a good computer and printer, and even the coffee is better. As long as people are productive, companies should let people work at home."[1]

The latest in affordable technology, from personal computers to fax machines, has enabled unprecedented numbers of people to work for others from their own home. With standard office equipment becoming the home-office standard, opportunities to telecommute are growing. It is becoming ever more popular as companies clamor to find new ways to work and employees search for new ways to integrate work with family life. Many jobs can be done at home from a full-time or part-time basis as an independent contractor for someone else, if entrepreneurship or telecommuting isn't your cup of tea.

A man from Boise, Idaho, decided to change his life when he set up a computer, a phone line, a modem, a printer, and a facsimilie machine in a spare bedroom. Instead of fighting traffic in the morning, he now checks in with his company by computer before 8:00 A.M., when the rates are lower, and receives messages through an electronic mail system. This telecommuter isn't alone; a large number of companies are now beginning to implement work-at-home plans. By 1990 approximately 500 companies had some kind of telecommuting program and 1000 to 1500 had an informal approach to employees working at home. Because so many companies nationwide have an informal option for some of their employees, it is difficult to determine just how many telecommuters there actually are. A growing number of professionals also work at home—an estimated 13 million. The number has grown 50 percent in the last ten years, and it is projected to grow another 50 percent in the next decade.[2] One thing is certain—the number of people working at home for others is growing rapidly.

Many small companies have adopted casual work-at-home programs. Some large corporations, however, have adopted a formal telecommuting program, including BankAmerica, J.C. Penney, Travelers Insurance, American Express, Honeywell, and Pacific Bell.[3] IBM has changed its personnel policy to allow mothers who have had children within the last three years to do some work at home. (IBM is trying to determine what kinds of problems it will encounter and whether a home-based employee program is a viable option for the future.) The City and County of Los Angeles, as well as the State of California, have implemented a telecommuting pilot program. (The County program hopes to include up to 2000 of its 17,000 employees over the next few years.) Even the Air Force and the Federal Government may be joining the telecommuting bandwagon.

When Pacific Bell moved its headquarters 40 miles from where it had been in San Francisco, many of the white-collar workers did not want to make the move, so they implemented a part-time telecommuting program. Now a large number of the employees work away from the office one or two days a week. After the October 1989 earthquake in San Francisco (which brought temporary gridlock to the Bay area), Pacific Bell allowed them to stay away three or four days. Since then, interest in telecommuting has been piqued in some companies. Many of them are further examining how telecommuting might work for them. As cities become more and more congested, telecommuting is becoming a way to keep people out of the traffic.

Working at home for others is also a viable option for the disabled, the handicapped, single parents, mothers who want extended maternity leave, and many retired people who still want to work. Not all of the elderly are content to just needlepoint and play golf! The SBA reported that an American Association of Retired Persons (AARP) survey found there are "four to five million retired older persons who would prefer paid employment, but only if they had flexible hours, no journey to work, and other criteria that suggest home-based work."[4] Since people are living longer and retiring earlier, this segment of the population is growing rapidly. Some companies are actively trying to hire retired persons. Some are even offering personal computer training. SeniorNet is a nonprofit organization and electronic network that trains people 55 and over to use a personal computer. SeniorNet has over 30 locations nationwide. They use volunteer seniors as teachers to make technology available to senior citizens. This has enabled some of them to reenter the job market. One 82-year-old woman came to their classes, furthered that knowledge at her community college, and then got a part-time job.

Both companies and employees can benefit from a telecommuting program. The companies don't have to pay overhead for these employees, turnover can be cut down, and productivity can be increased by as much as 20 to 60 percent. Some companies can expand even without physical space by letting employees go home. Many home-based businesses can grow this way without being forced to find office space by hiring other home-basers. I worked for a company for a short time that did this. I was working half my time at the office and half my time at home. When new employees were added, space became a scarce commodity, so I jumped at the chance to work strictly at home. I was still an employee, still got my paycheck every Friday, and still had my company benefits. In fact that very situation is what eventually led me to my own home business.

Many jobs can be done just as well at home as they can in the office, from data entry to actually running a company. Salaried home-based workers often include accountants, salespeople, researchers, bookkeepers, writers, insurance agents, data entry personnel, lawyers, artists, stockbrokers, telemarketing representatives, word processors, and many others.

Telecommuting works best when people have jobs where productivity can be measured. Companies must break the mold of "I must see my employees to effectively manage them." Even though many managers have difficulty supervising absent employees, the quality of the work they produce will tell if they are working at home effectively. If you need to punch a time clock for the boss to know whether you are giving your all, you will have trouble. If your boss or corporation cannot see past the time report, no matter what your output is, telecommuting will be difficult. Surveys have found that telecommuting is difficult for people whose jobs mean they must deal directly with people in a managerial capacity, or attend frequent meetings, or work on computers tied to mainframes, as well as for those in purchasing or building management.[5]

Gil Gordon (of Gil Gordon and Associates) has founded a business based on the telecommuting trend. He consults with organizations to help them implement telecommuting programs, and says that most companies select telecommuters from within their current in-office workforce. Telecommuting employers look for people who possess some of the same characteristics as entrepreneurs. They want people who can meet their deadlines, are disciplined, and are self-motivated. They want their employees to have worked out childcare arrangements, and to have enough space at home to do the work. They are also looking for people who do not need the social atmosphere of the office environment to be happy in their work.

If you want to work at home for someone else, consider this:

- First, look for a type of job that's not time-dependent—a job that can be done at any time during the day or night when you have the time available.

- Second, set a realistic goal about the number of hours you can actually work. Depending on the age and number of your children, this can vary from full-time to just a few hours a week. Gordon says, "A lot of people have been burned by setting unrealistic expectations for themselves. Ask yourself, 'How late do I want to stay up at night doing this?'" When you're burning the midnight oil for someone else, it's easy to get resentful. Determine beforehand just how much you want to work.

- Third, consider the availability of another childcare provider, whether your spouse, your grandma, or a neighbor. When you work for other people you are subject to their demands, and most employers prefer that the childcare issue not hinder your work for them. Working at home for someone else while raising children can be more trying than working for yourself because you have someone other than yourself to please. Your boss will expect a certain quota and quality of work. If you do not meet his expectations because of the juggling act between your kids and your work, you won't be working for him very long. If you're going to be working full-time, decide before you start what kind of childcare help you will have. Doing two full-time jobs at once means that neither job gets your best.

Ways to Work at Home for Others

1. *Approach your current or former employer.* If you have a good track record, and your job can be done at home, you may be able to negotiate a work-at-home position. Prove yourself as an employee, and volunteer to take special projects or part of your work home occasionally. Let management see the effectiveness of this method. You might propose working at home on an extended project or for part of your work week. When you have demonstrated that your job actually can be done from home effectively, then propose your work-at-home plan to your boss. If you are not employed or your present job cannot be done at home, begin looking for another salaried position that might be done from home, and

try to sell a new employer on your idea. Tell as many people as you can that you are looking for this type of work.

2. *Look for a subcontracting arrangement.* A subcontractor works at home without owning his own business, but works for those who do. If you don't have a current or former employer with which to work out a work-at-home arrangement, how do you find the companies that are doing this? Gil Gordon says, "Shoe leather research!" Companies, as a rule, do not advertise work-at-home positions. Tell people that you are looking for a subcontracting arrangement. Talk with business owners in the field in which you want to work. Try to get a feel for who is doing the type of work you are interested in and who might need some help.

Check out available resources, such as *The Work at Home Sourcebook*, by Lynie Arden, which lists companies that have telecommuting programs and describes how to find such jobs.

The continued growth of home-based work will depend a lot on how businesses react to this trend. Hopefully more and more companies will see the potential of using home-based workers who are full-fledged employees of their corporations. The future of successful telecommuting programs rests in the hands of employees and company decision-makers. Employees should continue to lobby for the work-at-home option, proposing formal or informal programs to their employers. Company executives should discover what many other progressive companies already have—that telecommuting and part-time or full-time work from home as an employee is not only viable, but is beneficial for the company as well as the employee.

Employees Versus Independent Contractors

If you work for someone else at home, be careful of the way in which you are paid and treated by your employer. Are you an employee or an independent contractor? There are many companies that treat their workers as employees but pay them as independent contractors. You are an employee if someone other than you controls how and when you work. You are an independent contractor if you decide the terms of your work arrangements and can work for more than one company. (Some contract consultants, who consult with one company for a period of time, are limited to working strictly for that company for the duration of their contract, but are then free to take on new clients.)

A plumber might be an independent contractor. He might have his own tools, call his own shots, decide how to do the work, and have multiple clients. Compare that to someone who does word processing at home 30 or 40 hours a week for the same word-processing bureau. That agency assigns the work, tells the worker how to do it, checks his work, and sets his rate of pay. That person is an employee. However, if that word-processing person worked for someone who allowed him to work at home if he wanted to, could work for others, could accept or turn down jobs at will without jeopardizing his position, and was not told specific hours or ways in which he must work, then for all practical purposes he would be an independent contractor.

Some people don't mind being paid on a contract basis. They have nothing taken out of their checks, so they get more money on the front end. Sometimes both parties are happy with this arrangement, but the IRS has said that it doesn't matter what the two parties agree to. The danger is not necessarily that home-workers are going to be exploited and paid less than a traditional worker, since some home-workers say they are earning as much as or more than their office counterparts on a per-hour basis. However, they are not getting the matching contributions from Social Security, the unemployment insurance coverage, or in some cases, worker's compensation protection. Not only could the employer get into trouble for this, but it's benefit money out of the pocket of the worker—today's money as well as his retirement income, since the employer is not matching the Social Security payments and the percentage that the employee pays is higher than the amount that is deducted from an employee.

Beware of Fraudulent Homeworking Opportunities

There are many ads in newspapers and magazines that promise the moon for the price of peanuts. "Home-workers Wanted: Big Profits. No Experience." "Envelope Stuffing. Big Money." Think about it—would employers really let others in on big profits without either experience or an investment? Here's how the scheme works: People place those phony ads looking for people who want to work at home and strike it rich. You just "send $15.00 for more information." What you receive are details on how to set up a business like theirs, defrauding other people. You would then invest in stamps, envelopes, and other items, and buy advertisements in which you would request other unsuspecting people to send you money "for more information." In these schemes there is no actual job at issue.

In other schemes, people propose to pay you a certain amount for each envelope you stuff for them. You must then buy their fliers and pay for your own ads at your expense, asking others to send you a self-addressed stamped envelope for more information on how to earn money at home. After you receive a certain quota of these envelopes, you stuff them and give them to your employer for payment. This type of job requires you to spend your own funds and depends on the number of responses to your ads—not a great way to make a living!

The U.S. Postal Service Investigation Service has said, "In practically all businesses, envelope stuffing has become a highly mechanized operation using sophisticated mass mailing techniques and equipment which eliminates any profit potential for an individual doing this type of work at home. The Inspection Service knows of no work-at-home promotion that ever produces income as alleged."[6] That Service, incidentally, put over 3500 of these fraudulent operations out of business! Other ads for home-based work ask you to send money, but all you may get is a list of firms that use home-workers. You must then contact each firm individually.

The old saying that "if it sounds too good to be true, it probably is" holds true for home-working advertisements. If they ask you to send them money, beware. Most people are paid by their employer, not the other way around. Investigate before you invest. Do a little research. See if the company's phone number is listed with directory assistance, and call to see if anyone answers during business hours. Call the Better Business Bureau in your area, and the city listed in the ad, if you have questions. If you are (or suspect you are) a victim of mail fraud, write to Mail Fraud, Chief Postal Inspector, Postal Inspection Services, Washington, D.C. 20260, or to the Postal Inspector in care of the city in the ad.

There may be some reputable mass-mailing companies that hire home-workers, but get these leads from the yellow pages, not the classifieds. Don't send them money, and check for a local phone number, not a post office box number.

Take-Out Work

Many people who have traditional office jobs also spend some time working for their employers at home.

According to studies, this so-called take-out work is done in order to avoid interruptions, to meet deadlines, to make up for lack of time at the office, and to allow the worker to be with his or her family more often. A survey done by *Modern Office Technology* found that 95 percent of the respondents had taken work home in the previous year, and that 39 percent bring it home at least once a week. Companies often help employees by purchasing or helping them purchase equipment for their home offices. (Almost 77 percent of take-out workers have companies that pay for products and equipment to work at home.) The number of people using computers at home for business was up 28 percent in 1987, and 35 percent of Americans who work at home own a personal computer.[7]

Bill Mattox with the Family Research Council says, "I think one of the things we like to be encouraging is not only more home-based work, where people work almost exclusively out of the home in some type of business, but also more take-out work, where workers who have families want to organize their lives around their family's schedule rather than organizing their family schedules around work."

13

Tax Aspects of a Home Business

As a home-business owner, there are certain tax advantages to which you are entitled. The purpose of this chapter is not to provide legal advice, but to alert you to some issues you might not be aware of. Please consult your accountant, tax preparer, CPA, or other tax professional for advice in your home business, as the tax law changes almost as quickly as Congress changes its mind.

Take Your Deductions

Deductions are costs incurred by an enterprise (including more than just cash expenses) while you are doing business that are used to reduce sales or revenue in calculating the profits of an enterprise that are taxable. You want to lower the amount of taxes you pay Uncle Sam? Take all the deductions you have coming to you.

The Home-Office Deduction

The home business provides the taxpayer with an opportunity for a deduction generally not otherwise available: a deduction for the business use of your home. However, the workplace in your home must meet certain IRS criteria. For example, the part of your home utilized as a workplace must be used regularly and exclusively as one of the following:

1. Your principal place of business.

2. A place to meet or deal with your clients or customers in the normal course of your trade or business. If this is the qualifying criterion you are using, the IRS requires that you must physically meet with clients or customers on your premises, and your meetings with them must be substantial and integral to the conduct of your business. Occasional meetings and telephone calls are not enough.

3. If the part of your home used as a workplace is a separate structure and is not attached to your house or residence.

By *regular* use of your home-office, the IRS means that it is not just used incidentally or occasionally, but with frequency. *Exclusive* use means that the part of your home used for business must be used *only* for business, unless you use your home in providing daycare services or for inventory storage, where the exclusive-use rule does not apply. If you are working at home for an employer, and want to claim the home-office deduction, you must be able to substantiate that the use of your home is for the convenience of your employer.

Direct and Indirect Expenses

The deduction for the business use of your home involves two types of expenses—direct expenses and indirect expenses.

A *direct expense* is any directly identifiable expense made for the portion of the home used for business. Examples include:

Painting the office

Buying a new rug for it

Light bulbs

Office repairs and maintenance

Indirect expenses are expenses incurred for your entire home which must then be allocated between your personal and business use. Examples of this type of expenses include:

Utilities (Gas, electricity, telephone service, etc.)

Property and liability insurance

Real estate taxes

Depreciation

Rent (you don't have to own a house to get the deduction)

To determine the portion of the indirect expense that you can deduct, you must define the part of the home used for business as opposed to the rest of the home. Simply determine what percentage of your home is used for business by dividing the square footage of your office space by the total square footage of your home. For example, if you have a 1600-square-foot home and you have a 160-square-foot room set up for business, this would represent 10 percent of the home. You would then be able to deduct 10 percent of all of your indirect expenses.

The deduction for indirect expenses is limited to the gross income from your business after you subtract the following:

1. the business portion of otherwise-deductible mortgage interest, real estate taxes, and casualty and theft losses, and—

188 / Tax Aspects of a Home Business

2. other business expenses not attributable to the use of your home.

For further explanation you can request publication #587: *The Business Use of Your Home* from the IRS.

Regular Business Deductions

Other deductions available to home businesses are those generally defined as regular business deductions. These are expenses normally deductible by any business, not just those in the home. They include:

- Advertising
- Answering service
- Business use of your car
- Courier
- Depreciation
- Equipment rental, lease, or repair
- Insurance
- Interest
- Legal and professional services
- Office supplies
- Postage
- Travel, meals, and entertainment
- Wages paid to employees, contract workers, spouse, or children
- Publications or books related to your business
- Membership fees for business organizations

- Business gifts
- Delivery charges
- Printing costs
- Taxes
- Long-distance calls
- Licenses and permits
- Education expenses (workshops, classes, seminars, etc., necessary for your business)
- Any materials directly related to the operation of your business or production of your product.

Keep good records so that you can take all the deductions available to you, and so you will be able to substantiate your claims in case of an audit. Save all your receipts. If you incur a business expense and do not get a receipt, handwrite one.

When recording your business mileage, be sure to not only list the number of miles traveled and the date, but include your destination. When recording your entertainment expenses, include the amount and date of the expense, the place, the persons in attendance, and the relationship to you of those persons. Just saving restaurant stubs or credit-card receipts is not enough validation of your business entertainment expenses to please the IRS.

Estimated Tax Payments

If you are self-employed in your home, another tax consideration is to determine if you need to make quarterly estimated tax payments. As a self-employed person, you have no employer to withhold taxes from your pay, so the burden falls on you.

Basically, you must make estimated tax payments if you meet all three of the following qualifications. (If you fail to make these payments, you may be charged a penalty.)

1. If you expect to owe $500 or more for the year (in excess of any withholding or tax credits).

2. If you don't expect your income tax withholding and credits to be at least 90 percent of your tax due for the year.

3. If you don't expect your income tax withholding and credits to equal your tax paid last year.

Estimated tax payments are due on the following dates: April 15 (for January through March), June 15 (for April through May), September 15 (for June through August), and January 15 (of the next year) (for September through December).

Hiring an accountant or attorney is probably a lot cheaper than not hiring one. If you establish a relationship with him or her early in your business, he will be available to help you when the need arises. You should also establish a good relationship with your banker. These professionals can lend their expertise in areas unfamiliar to you, thus saving you money, aggravation, and legal problems.

14

Keeping the Right Perspective

There are some things in life that demand our highest priority: our relationship with the Lord, our relationship with our spouse and our children, and our work. Working from home provides an excellent opportunity to make a living while keeping those priorities in proper perspective. It certainly isn't the easiest route to take, but is one that can bless you immeasurably. God can use your home business to teach you spiritual lessons in ways that you never dreamed possible.

There will be days when you get started at the crack of dawn and find yourself working long after you want to quit. There will be days when it appears that nothing is going right: The children are demanding, your spouse is demanding, and your clients need you. You may feel guilty over lack of time with your family, your household responsibilities, or your work. You may even begin to question why you started this business in the first place.

But even though these days may happen occasionally, you can be victorious as the Lord sustains you. Barbara has seen that happen frequently while working from home: "Whenever I wonder if this is all worth it, the Lord reconfirms it in small ways."

Working at home is not for everyone. Not all people have the temperament or desire to start a business of their own. Many do not have the family support needed to do so. Others do not have the energy level or drive necessary to make it work. And some simply are not called to do it.

If you do not feel that the Lord has called you to work at home, don't even try it. Without His guidance in your endeavor, and your commitment to fulfill His plan in your life, your business could end up at the bottom of the broken-business statistics. Doug Sherman and William Hendricks say in *Your Work Matters to God*, "Unless you can make a connection between what you do all day and what you think God wants you to be doing, you will never find ultimate meaning in your work or in your relationship with God." Don't just start a business for the sake of having a business. Know beforehand that what you are doing is part of the Lord's plan for your life.

Bigger than the Problems

The blessings can overshadow the problems. Being an entrepreneur and a Christian is a lesson in trust. God has used Heidi's business to teach her and her husband that very thing. She explains, "My business hasn't taken off extremely well in terms of superabundance coming in, but it's taught us a lot about relying on the Lord. Sometimes just in the nick of time some business will come in. I'm not the super-salesperson, and I tend to want to stay home more than go out and solicit business, so God's hand has really been evident in bringing business in. God has taught us trust."

The blessings not only lift us up but also lighten our load, strengthen our faith, and teach us about the nature of our Creator as He gives to us from His storehouse. Working from my home has been exciting because I have seen the Lord working in my life in very concrete ways.

I have found that the Lord has a way of hearing our innermost desires even when we don't fall on our knees and petition for them fervently. Some people have difficulty working as much as they need to in their businesses, while others work too much. There have been times when I have fallen into both categories. The Lord used one such time to teach me a few things.

My business had taken off like gangbusters, leaving me extremely busy. As the business grew, I had less time available to be the kind of wife and mother I desired. Without realizing how it had happened or how I could get off the whirlwind track, I had become immersed in my business. There were still plenty of times when the kids and I made cookies, read books, and played (since two days a week I was both full-time Mom and home-business owner), but their place on the priority list had slipped. Those things were left for my "free time," after all my business obligations were met. Sometimes I would find myself in the middle of chocolate-chip cookie batter and preschool chatter, with my mind dwelling on my latest project instead of enjoying the moment with my kids. Since I am a pretty motivated, ambitious person by nature (as are many entrepreneurs) my work was never done. I always came up with something else to do regarding the business. This was changing the nature of my time with the children. Gradually I began to notice that on the three weekdays that our housekeeper/baby-sitter came, I went into my office and said, "Mommy has to work now; go ask Miss Ida," even if there wasn't a deadline looming. I slowly saw this happening and hated it, but I wasn't sure how to change it. I reasoned, "If Ida is going to be here, I need to get as much done as possible. If I work while she's here I can increase my business, which we need, and I can still have free time with the kids when I'm done. Besides, I'm home with them. It's not like I'm off at an office or anything."

A Lesson in Trust

As I began to see the disparity between my time with the children and my need to work in the business, I felt stuck. How could I just slow down on my own when we needed the money? How would my husband feel? He didn't really *see* anything wrong. Because my helper was here so much, the house was always clean, the meals were served on time, and there was always plenty of clean underwear (which wasn't always the case when I was trying to do everything myself). What he *couldn't* see was the time I spent in the same house with the children while I was totally removed from what they were doing or feeling—all for the sake of the business. I began to pray for a way to be a better mother to them and to return to the values I treasure. As usual, the Lord knew the desire of my heart.

Slowly, one by one, my clients began to drop off. I wasn't doing anything differently to warrant this decrease as far as I could tell, but I had fewer and fewer jobs. The housekeeper was no longer affordable, because with less business there was less money. On the other hand, the less business I had, the more time I had. Business consultants would probably have told me to invest that time in my business and promote my company back into success. But I didn't. I had been wanting to spend more time with my children anyway, so I was thrilled to have an excuse to be with them more. I began to get reacquainted with Slap Jack and Candyland!

My five-year-old and I started doing housework together, something that had previously been done in the quickest way possible. She collected and sorted laundry, cleaned the tub, washed the mirrors and her babies' faces with Windex, ran the vacuum cleaner for the first time, learned how to use a dustpan, saw how much soap is used on a load of laundry, and helped with an assortment of other tasks. For her this was a fun new game. I was ashamed that I had taken so little time before this to teach her these things and to do them with her at a relaxed pace.

The kids also began to accompany me—often. They went with me to occasional client meetings and learned quickly what was acceptable behavior and what wasn't. On one trip that resulted in an extremely long wait, we made use of our time by talking and reading books. Right when I thought they were going to lose their patience with the wait, Jacquelyn looked up at me and said, "Mom, you're fun!" My heart melted. All my children really wanted was my time, and I had been far too stringent in the amount I gave them. I praised God that He had brought me back to what was important through the slowing down of my business.

For my husband and me this was a lesson in trust and priorities, because even though I now had more "Mommy-time," we still needed the income. (Facing a possible business loss is a scary thing.) The thought of an outside job for me with daycare for the kids was even scarier. But instead of getting ulcers about losing the business, we decided to take Paul's advice: "Be anxious for nothing, but in everything by prayer and supplication with thanksgiving let your requests be made known to God" (Philippians 4:6).

Keeping the Right Perspective

We began to pray that the Lord would meet our financial needs and direct us with the business. I'd like to tell you that we prayed and I got ten new regular clients the next day or that we won the Publisher's Clearinghouse sweepstakes, but that didn't happen. It took a period of several months before we really saw God's answer to our prayers. The Lord used that time to show us that He would meet our needs on a daily basis. There was no doubt that the Lord had "cleared my slate" for some things that were coming in my life. I would never have been able to orchestrate the timing of the events or organize the details like God did. He also knew that I needed the time to make my children a top priority again, and to be available for future tasks. God taught me that I had been depending on my *business* to make ends meet instead of on *God Himself*. I learned that what really mattered was my obedience and availability to the Lord, and my time with my family.

Now here's where the miracle part comes in. All of a sudden, and with no doing on my own, I began to get new business. I had actually gotten down to zero clients (now that's rock bottom!) when the phone began to ring off the wall. Strangely, every single job I received was through word-of-mouth advertising and not a result of any of my efforts. My business income soon doubled from that of previous months, and I knew the increase was truly from the Lord.

It's difficult for me to admit that I had trouble making time for my children like I should have, and that my business has been less than the "home-business model," but I think I struggle with some of the same things you do. It's called "losing your perspective," and it's very easy to do. Even if you don't have children, be careful to keep the right perspective. Remember to make time for the things in life that really matter. Having a home business is not always easy, and sometimes it's downright tough. But it's worth it, because the Lord will see us through and direct us in our work, through both adversity and victory.

Success Is from God

Brenda has realized in her business time and time again, "No matter how hard I push, I can't make things happen unless it's the Lord's will. I'm finally approaching the business the way we should approach everything in life. I'm going to be obedient to the Lord, but what happens beyond that is His business. He can do it, but I can't."

In a letter to "Focus on the Family" radio talkshow listeners, Dr. James Dobson described how success truly is from God. "Egos being what they are, the natural inclination is to take personal credit for any successes coming our way. But we know the dangers of that error. Every positive thing that has happened in our 12-year history has been a direct consequence of God's blessing. If He ever removes His hand of mercy from us, we would flounder helplessly in a sea of futility."[1]

Karen has seen the importance of God's timing and plan in her appliqué business. When she first started her sole proprietorship, she envisioned herself with a small appliqué company with about four or five women sewing for her. She soon realized that there was quite a demand for her work, and her business began to grow. She advertised in a major metropolitan newspaper for more contract workers, but she got only two responses to her ad. Some time later, after much prayer about the direction the Lord was leading her business, she had an opportunity to take on a tremendous volume of work. She had to either turn it down or hire more help. She tried an ad in the same paper again, and this time more than three times as many people called than she could even interview! Her small circle of sewers grew to over 75 women, whom she gave work to so they could work out of their homes as well. Many of those women are homemakers and mothers who want to be at home with their children. By being obedient and available to the Lord, not only was Karen and her family blessed, but she in turn was able to be a blessing to the lives of 75 women and their families. Remember, God can use us when we least expect it.

Many women who start home businesses also value their role as wife, mother, and homemaker. Don't think that you must be any less in any of these areas just because you decide to work out of your home. You will need to adjust a great deal, but don't think that one role precludes the other. Titus 2:5 tells us that we must be "sensible, pure, workers at home, kind, being subject to

[our] own husbands, that the word of God may not be dishonored." Study the godly woman in Proverbs 31. That lady would have fit in nicely in this decade, for she was on the move and got things done. She cooked, served, bought real estate, invested, and helped the needy. She was a seamstress, a beltmaker, and a popular mother with her children. Yet she remained a virtuous woman, an excellent wife. Let her be your role model.

If you feel the Lord is leading you to begin working at home, but are fearful because of a previous business failure or past mistakes, don't let that alone hinder you from beginning. Successful people also have failures—lots of them. The legendary Babe Ruth struck out 1330 times, yet ended up being the greatest home-run hitter in the history of baseball! If you've struck out, don't dwell on past errors. "Brethren, I do not regard myself as having laid hold of it yet; but one thing *I do*; forgetting what lies behind and reaching forward to what lies ahead..." (Philippians 3:13).

True Commitment

The cornerstone of home-business success is based on one word: commitment. Commitment to the business and to the Lord.

If we are not committed to the work we do, we flounder. That commitment is based on dedication. Without that dedication we are simply marking time instead of learning, growing, and prospering. Commitment takes work. It takes our energy, our time, our concentration, and our determination for success. If it didn't, we wouldn't be seeing the tremendous number of divorces that we do, for successful marriages are also based on commitment. Be committed to your work, not just to reap the benefits but because your work really does matter to God.

We must also commit our work, our goals, and our lives to the Lord. The Bible has a lot to say about commitment. One of the most meaningful verses to me while I was starting my business was Proverbs 16:3: "Commit your works to the Lord, and your plans will be established." The business is His, to be used for His glory. Psalm 37:3-5 tells us, "Trust in the Lord, and do good; dwell in the land and cultivate faithfulness. Delight yourself in the Lord, and He will give you the desires of your heart. Commit your way to the Lord, trust also in Him, and He will do it." We are to trust and delight in the Lord, and commit our goals to Him. If we do that, God will honor our commitment. Most of all, we are to commit our lives to Him. It is difficult to commit anything to God if we have never made Him Lord of our lives. He wants to give us the desires of our hearts and to establish our plans, but He requires that we have made Him our Lord. If you have never done that, I pray that before you consider anything else, you consider Jesus. He wants a personal relationship with you, and will actively intervene in your life if you invite Him in. Make a difference not only in your business but also in your eternal future by making your commitment to Him.

As you begin your journey into the home-business realm, you will learn and you will grow, but most of all you will realize the power of the Lord at work in your life like never before. Be attuned to all the miracles that God will do for you which you might otherwise miss. If you really feel the Lord leading you to begin your business, He will amaze you with the direct interaction He lovingly gives when asked. God cares about the very smallest detail in our lives.

Remember that this is an adventure to be all that you can for the Lord. Commit your work to Him, and He will establish your plans. Let that be the motto of your enterprise. If you have doubts in your business (and you will), rest in the Lord. If you have fears about what you are doing (and you may), trust in your heavenly Father. When you see victories, give God the praise. Let working at home be a way to honor and serve the Lord. Allow God to use your work at home to make your family, personal, work, and spiritual life be all that God wants it to be. Above all, remember that God sees possibilities above all that we ask or think.

I pray that the Lord will bless you in your new endeavor!

"May He grant you your heart's desire and fulfill all your counsel" (Psalm 20:4).

Resources:
Where to Go for Help

There is a wealth of information available to assist you in starting a home business. Consider the following.

Community Sources of Information

Local libraries, colleges, universities, and chambers of commerce provide a wealth of information to those willing to dig it out. Also, check your phone directory to inquire about business groups in your community. Check for local chapters of national organizations.

The Copyright Office

This is a good source for many free publications.

Register of Copyrights
Library of Congress
Washington, D.C. 20559
204-287-9100

The Internal Revenue Service

Publication #587, *Business Use of Your Home*, is vital to determine the amount of your home that can be written off for tax purposes. It outlines use requirements and rules on deductions.

Also available:

Determining Whether a Worker Is an Employee, #SS-8
Index to Tax Publications, #900

Tax Guide for Small Business, #334

Write to:

> Superintendent of Documents
> U.S. Government Printing Office
> Washington, D.C. 20402

PASS (Procurement Automated Source System)

This is a computerized listing of firms with the SBA, and can assist the small-business person in procuring work. Registered small businesses can be considered for federal contracts and subcontracts when they sign up with PASS. For more information write to:

> U.S. Small Business Administration
> 1441 L Street N.W.
> Washington, D.C. 20416

Procurement Assistance

The SBA offers many services to help the small-business person get government contracts, including set-asides (contracts reserved specifically for small and/or disadvantaged businesses), subcontracting opportunities, and PASS. Contact your local SBA office or call 204-653-6586.

SCORE (Service Corps of Retired Executives)

This SBA program provides training and free management counseling through retired and active business professionals nationwide. There are over 750 SCORE locations nationwide with 13,000 counselors advising people who want to go into business or helping those already doing so. This service is free and confidential. For a small fee, SCORE also sponsors workshops on how to start up new businesses or on specialized subjects. The background of the counselors is on record, so you can request a counselor to fit your particular need. Counselors will stay with you as long as necessary. SCORE is listed in the blue pages of your telephone book under "U.S. Government" and the subheading of "Small Business Administration."

Small Business Administration

The U.S. Small Business Administration offers assistance to those in small business, providing financial help, management assistance, help in obtaining government contracts, counseling services, and a library of low-cost publications. (See especially SBA Publication #MP 15, *The Business Plan for Home-Based Business*.) Most local offices can provide you with a free business start-up kit. Look in the "Government" section of your phone book for your local SBA office. You may also write to:

> U.S. Small Business Administration
> P.O. Box 15454
> Fort Worth, Texas 76119

Small Business Answer Desk

For a quick overview of how the SBA can help you, call the Small Business Answer Desk toll-free at 1-800-368-5855. Recorded information is provided on the following topics:

1. Starting a Small Business

2. Financing a Small Business

3. SCORE (Service Corps of Retired Executives)

4. SBA Services and Local Assistance

5. Facts on Small Businesses and Business Data

The information you hear is recorded, but you can also talk with a business counselor personally. To get a counselor on the line you must call between 9 A.M. and 5 P.M. Eastern time, Monday through Friday. You will be given local information on SBA offices, Small Business Development Centers, and SCORE offices in your area if you punch in your area code on a Touchtone phone.

Small Business Development Centers

These SBA centers provide low-cost assistance, counseling, and training to prospective and existing small-business owners in the area of growth, expansion, innovation, productivity, and management improvement. There are over 600 locations.

State Agencies

Most states have agencies that promote economic growth by assisting small businesses. Look in the phone directory under "Local and State Government." Many states also publish guides to starting a business in their state. They may also have a procurement program.

Women's Business Ownership, Office of

For help in starting or expanding a business, contact:

> U.S. Small Business Administration
> 1441 L Street N.W., Room 414
> Washington, D.C. 20416
> 204-653-4000

Publications from the IRS

Business Use of Your Home (IRS Publication #587). Annual.

Recordkeeping for a Small Business (IRS Publication #583).

Tax Guide for Small Business (IRS Publication #334).

Publications from the SBA (1441 L St., Washington, D.C. 20416)
Financial Management and Analysis

FM 1   ABC's of Borrowing

FM 2   Basic Budgets for Profit Planning

FM 4   Understanding Cash Flow

FM 5   A Venture Capital Primer for Small Business

FM 6   Accounting Services for Small Service Firms

MP 20   Business Continuation Planning

MP 21   Developing a Strategic Business Plan

MP 22   Inventory Management

MP 23   Techniques for Problem Solving

MP 24   Techniques for Productivity Improvement

MP 25   Selecting the Legal Structure for Your Business

MP 26   Evaluating Franchise Opportunities

MP 27   Starting a Retail Travel Agency

MP 28   Small Business Risk Management Guide

Published Literature

Anderson, Joan Westen. *Best of Both Worlds: A Guide to Home-Based Careers.* Crozet, VA: Betterway Publishing, 1982.

Arden, Lynie. *The Work-at-Home Sourcebook: How to Find "At-Home" Work That's Right for You.* Boulder, CO: Live Oak Publications, 1988.

Arthur, Julietta K. *How to Make a Home Business Pay.* Englewood Cliffs, NJ: Prentice Hall.
This is out of print, but available at many public libraries.

Behr, Marlon and Lazar, Wendy. *Women Working Home.* Edison, NJ: WWH Inc., 1983.

Bohigian, Valerie. *How to Make Your Home-Based Business Grow: Getting Bigger Profits from Your Product.* New York: New American Library, 1986.

Bohigian, Valerie. *Real Money from Home: How to Start, Manage and Profit from a Home Business Service.* New York: New American Library, 1985.

Bond, Larry K. *How to Make Money with a Home Computer.* Logan, UT: Bond Enterprises, 1986.

Golden, Bonnie J. *The Cottage Industry: Home-Based Businesses for Older Adults; An Information Guidebook.*

Bowker, Katie Muldoon. *Catalog Marketing: The Complete Guide.* New York: AMACOM, 1988.

Brabec, Barbara. *Crafts Marketing Success Secrets.* Crozet, VA: Betterway Publications, 1988.

Brabec, Barbara. *Creative Cash.* Crozet, VA: Betterway Publications, 1986.

Brabec, Barbara. *Help for Your Growing Homebased Business.* Naperville, IL: Barbara Brabec Productions, 1987. (P.O. Box 2138, Naperville, IL 60566.)

Brabec, Barbara. *Homemade Money*, 3rd ed. Crozet, VA: Betterway Publications, 1989.

Branson III, John J. *How to Start a Word Processing Business at Home.* New York: Simon and Schuster, Inc.

Cassell, Dana K. *Making Money with Your Home Computer.* New York: Dodd Mead and Co., 1984.

Christensen, Kathleen. *Women and Home-Based Work: The Unspoken Contract* (based on a survey for the National Project on Home-Based Work). New York: H. Holt and Co., 1988.

The Complete Work-at-Home Directory and Idea Book. Huntington, NY: E.A Morgan Publishing Co.

Cooke, Ronald J. *How to Make Big Money at Home.* Cheektowaga, NY: Eden Press (dist. by Univ. of Toronto Pr.), 1986.

Davidson, Jeffrey P. *Avoiding the Pitfalls of Starting Your Own Business.* New York: Walker and Co., 1988.

Delany, George and Sandra. *The #1 Home Business Book.* Cockeysville, MD: Liberty Publishing Co., 1981.

Directory of Wholesale Printing and Office Supplies Sources. Huntington, NY: E.A. Morgan Publishing Co. (Over 100 direct sources.)

Edwards, Paul and Sarah, with Goode, J.N. *How to Publish a Profitable Newsletter* (cassette tapes). Cherry Valley Press, P.O. Box 836, South Pasadena, CA 91030.

Edwards, Paul and Sarah. *The Marketing Manager.* Cherry Valley Press, P.O. Box 836, South Pasadena, CA 91030.

Edwards, Paul and Sarah. *Working from Home*, rev. ed. Los Angeles: J.P. Tarcher, Inc., 1987.

Ellentuck, Albert B. *Leventhol and Horwath Small Business Tax Planning Guide*. New York: Avon Books, 1987.

Everett, John and Crowe, Elizabeth Powell. *Information for Sale: How to Start and Operate Your Own Data Research Service*. Blue Ridge Summit, PA: Tab Books, Inc., 1988.

Fleming, Lisa. *Electronic Cottage Handbook #2, Making $$ with Your Home Computer*. Davis, CA: Fleming, Ltd., 1989.

John Kremer. *Formaides for Direct Response Marketing*. Fairfield, IA: Ad-Lib Publications, 1983.

Friedberg, Ardy. *Computer Freelancers Handbook: Moonlighting with Your Home Computer*. New York: New American Library Publishing, 1984.

Frohbieter-Mueller, Jo. *Stay Home and Mind Your Own Business*. Crozet, VA: Betterway Publications, 1987.

Glen, Peggy. *Word-Processing Profits at Home*. Huntington Beach, CA: Aames-Allen Publishing, 1983.

Goldstein, Jerome. *In Business for Yourself: A Guide to Starting a Small Business and Running It Your Way*. New York: Charles Scribner's Sons, 1982.

Handy, Jim. *How to Uncover Hidden Business Opportunities that Make Money*. New York: Prentice-Hall, 1983.

Hausman, Carl. *Moonlighting: 148 Great Ways to Make Money on the Side*. New York: Avon Books, 1989.

Home Offices and Workspaces. Menlo Park, CA: Sunset Editions, Sunset-Lane, 1986.

Hook, Peg. *A Mother's Guide to Starting a Business at Home*. Littleton, CO: Harbinger House, 1982.

How to Succeed in a Home Business, 1 hr. video. Lorimar Home Video, 1987.

Hudson, Howard Penn. *Publishing Newsletters*. New York: Charles Scribners Sons, 1982.

Kahn, Sharon and The Philip Lief Group. *101 Best Businesses to Start*. New York: Doubleday and Co., 1988.
Profiles many businesses suitable for running from home.

Kamoroff, Bernard. *Small Time Operation: How to Start Your Own Small Business, Keep Your Books, Pay Your Taxes, and Stay Out of Trouble*, rev. ed. Laytonville, CA: Bell Springs Publishing, 1989.

Kennedy, Joyce L. and Arden, Lynie. *Work-at-Home Jobs*. Rockville, MD: Sun Features Publishing, 1987.

Kern, Caralee Smith. *Planning Your Own Home Business*. Lincolnwood, IL: Natl Textbook Co., 1986. VGM Career Horizons.

Kilgo, Edith Flowers. *Money in the Cookie Jar*. Grand Rapids: Baker Book House, 1980.

King, Norman. *Turn Your House into a Money Factory Working at Home*. Columbus, GA: Quill Publishing, 1982.

Kishel, Gregory. *Dollars on Your Doorstep: The Complete Guide to Home-Based Businesses*. New York: John Wiley and Sons Publishing, 1984.

Kremer, John. *Directory of Book, Catalog, and Magazine Printers*, 4th ed. Fairfield, IA: Ad-Lib Publishing, 1987.

Kremer, Kiefer, and McIlvride. *Book Marketing Opportunities: A Directory*. Fairfield, IA: Ad-Lib Publishing, 1987.

Lant, Jeffrey. *Money Talks: The Complete Guide to Creating a Profitable Workshop or Seminar in Any Field*. Cambridge, MA: JLA Publications, 1988.

Legal Aspects of Small Business, special report no. X3305. Los Angeles: American Entrepreneurs Association, 1984.

Lias, Edward J. *Income from Your Home Computer*. Reston, VA: Reston Publishing Co., 1983.

Lieberoff, Allen J. *Climb Your Own Ladder: 101 Home Businesses that Can Make You Wealthy*. New York: Simon and Schuster, 1982.

Liebers, Arthur. *How to Start a Profitable Retirement Business.* Babylon, NY: Pilot Books, 1987.

McConnel, Patricia. *Women's Work-at-Home Handbook: Income and Independence with a Computer.* New York: Bantam Books, 1986.

Murray, Jean Wilson. *Starting and Operating a Word Processing Service.* Babylon, NY: Pilot Books, 1983.

Newman, Roger E. *How You Can Achieve Financial Independence in Mail Order Working Out of Your Home.* United Research Publishing, 1986.

Olmsted, Barney and Smith, Suzanne. *The Job Sharing Handbook.* Berkeley: Ten Speed Press, 1985.

Paradis, Adrian. *The Small Business Information Source Book.* Crozet, VA: Betterway Publications, 1987.

Parascandolo, Sal. *How to Build a Fortune Writing and Selling Information by Mail.* Long Island City, NY: Realm Hill House, 1985.

Pride, Mary. *All the Way Home.* Westchester, IL: Crossway Books/Good News, 1989.

Purcell, Paul E. *The Complete Guide to Homemade Income.* Los Angeles: R.P. and P. Publications, 1987. Price, Robin, Printer.

Ross, Marilyn and Tom. *How to Make Big Profits Publishing City and Regional Books.* Saguache, CO: Communication Creativity, 1987.

Rugge, Sue. *How to Make Money Doing Research with Your Computer* (2 tapes).

Scott, Robert. *How to Set Up and Operate Your Office at Home.* New York: Macmillian Publishing Co.

Scott, Robert. *Office at Home.* New York: Charles Scribner's Sons, 1985.
This is out of print, but available at many public libraries.

Shown, Janet. *Freelance Foodcrafting: How to Become Profitably Self-Employed in Your Own Creative Cooking Business.* Boulder, CO: Live Oak Publishing, 1983.

Silberstein, Judith and Benton, F. Warren. *Bringing High-Tech Home*. New York: John Wiley and Sons, 1985.

Silberstein, Judith A. *Bringing High Tech Home: How to Create a Computer-Based Home Office*. New York: John Wiley and Sons, 1985.

Simon, Julian. *Getting into the Mail Order Business*. New York: McGraw-Hill, 1984.

Simon, Julian. *How to Start and Operate a Mail Order Business*. New York: McGraw-Hill, 1987.

Smith, Allan. *How to Sell Your Homemade Creation*. Palm Beach Gardens, FL: Success Publishing, 1984.

Sroge, Maxwell. *How to Create Successful Catalogs*. Colorado Springs: Maxwell Sroge Publications, Inc., 1985.

Tips on Work-at Home Schemes, Consumer Information Series. Council of the Better Business Bureau.

Toffler, Alvin. *The Third Wave*. New York: William Morrow and Co., Inc., 1980.

Whitmeyer, Claude; Rasberry, Salli, Phillips, Michael. *Running a One-Person Business*. Berkeley: Ten Speed Press, 1988.

Yagor, Jan. *Making Your Office Work for You*. New York: Doubleday and Co., Inc., 1989

If these books are not available at your bookstore, they may be out of print, so check your library or interlibrary loan. If they are still unavailable, contact the publisher.

Various Other Sources

Edwards, Paul and Sarah. *Paul and Sarah Edwards' Complete Start-Up Kit for a Home Business with Your Computer*. Cherry Valley Press, Box 836, South Pasadena, CA 91030.

Entrepreneur
2392 Morse Ave.
P.O. Box 19787
Irvine, CA 92713-9787

Improving Your Business Ability from the American Entrepreneur Association (the parentheses denote the book reference):

Credit Consulting (X1321)

Developing a Business Plan (X3402)

Entrepreneurs Institute (3-volume set) (X3429)

Entrepreneurial Quiz (X1254)

How to Obtain Government Contracts (X1227)

Incorporation Kits for Any State (specify state) (X7000)

Legal Aspects of Small Business (X3305)

Lessons from America's Successful Enterpreneurs (X1327)

Personal Financial Planner (X1312)

SBA Loan Guide (X1315)

Standard Business Forms for the Entrepreneur (X1319)

SeniorNet
University of San Francisco
San Francisco, CA 94117-1080
415-666-6505

The Whole Work Catalog
The New Careers Center
6003 N. 51st
Box 297
Boulder, CO 80306

Associations

A note about trade associations:

A trade association is a group largely comprised of small-business people within a particular industry or service area. Such associations offer information about industry developments or trends, specialized publications about your field, information or educational opportunities in your area, management assistance, and sometimes lobbying for federal or state information regarding your field. Check your library and the *Encyclopedia of Associations* for groups in your particular industry or service.

American Business Management
P.O. Box 111
West Hyannis Port, MA 02671
1-800-333-4508

Offers assistance with tax issues for part-time and home businesses. Offers members certified public accounting and financial planning help, and help in case of an audit. Specializes in people who are part-timers.

American Home Business Association
397 Post Road
Darien, CT 06820
203-655-4380
1-800-433-6361, 1-800-441-2929
Newsletter—*Home BusinessLine*

Provides information for home-based businesses. Tax and legal professionals, as well as entrepreneurs, contribute to the newsletter. Members can get group insurance and discount travel packages. Also operates a buying service which offers discounted prices on office equipment and supplies.

American Woman's Economic
Development Corporation (AWED)
60 E. 42nd Street, Suite 405
New York, NY 10165
1-800-222-AWED
(in New York, 1-800-442-AWED)

AWED offers a hot line and telephone counseling service. It is staffed by 18 volunteer business professionals to advise women in any phase of business. A 90-minute telephone or in-person session costs $35.00. Quick questions can be answered in a ten-minute, $10.00 session.

Association of Part-Time Professionals
Row General Building
7655 Old Springhouse Road
McLean, VA 22012
703-734-7975

Promotes employment opportunities for men and women interested in part-time professional positions. Represents permanent part-timers, job-sharers, freelancers, consultants, and all part-time professionals. Annual membership is $45.00 initially, $35.00 each following year.

Home Business Resource Center
P.O. Box 115023-233
Carrollton, TX 75011

This resource center is this author's enterprise. It is an information clearinghouse dedicated to serving and encouraging home businesses. We provide resource information, books, and a newsletter *(HomeWork)* written from a Christian worldview.

Home By Choice, Inc.
Box 103
Vienna, VA 22183
703-281-6334

This is a national Christian organization, with members in 29 states, for mothers who choose to stay home. The goal is to provide encouragement and practical help for mothers at home. It has been recognized by the Bush administration as one of 200 family organizations in America. Annual membership is $15.00, which includes a bimonthly newsletter.

Mother's Home Business Network
P.O. Box 423
East Meadow, NY 11554
514-997-7394

Offers advice and support services plus information on home business products and services for mothers with home businesses.

Mothers At Home
P.O. Box 2208
Merrifield, VA 22116

This organization encourages and supports stay-at-home moms through its newsletter. It strives to boost the morale and image of mothers at home, and provides a forum for information exchange.

National Association for
the Cottage Industry
P.O. Box 14460
Chicago, IL 60614
312-472-8116

This association acts as an advocacy group for cottage workers and provides information on business organization methods, marketing and promotion, zoning, and government reports. It also advocates laws that would be helpful to home-based workers.

National Association of
Home-Based Businesses
P.O. Box 30220
Baltimore, MD 21270
301-363-3698

Encourages the creation of home-based businesses and works to discover new markets. Also offers seminars on starting and marketing your business.

The National Association for
the Self-Employed
2316 Gravel Rd.
Ft. Worth, TX 76118
817-589-2475
1-800-232-NASE

This is geared to self-employed small independent business persons. Promotes political awareness and conducts educational programs. Offers members travel, insurance, and legal services.

National Association of Women
Business Owners (NAWBO)
600 S. Federal Street, Suite 400
Chicago, IL 60605
312-922-0465

Serves as an information clearinghouse for women business owners, and offers workshops and seminars. Also offers education, management, and technical assistance. Has 38 local chapters. Membership is limited to women already in business.

National Association of Women's
Yellow Pages, Inc.
P.O. Box 87524
Chicago, IL 60680
312-470-2520

Publishes directories listing women-owned businesses and women's organizations. Will assist you in starting a directory of your own or in being listed.

National Chamber of Commerce for Women
Committee: Women in Home Based Businesses
Ten Waterside Plaza, Suite 6H
New York, NY 10010
212-685-3454

Works with local, regional, and state development agencies to expand business opportunities for women. Conducts pay comparisons.

The National Federation of Business and
Professional Women's Clubs, Inc. (BPW/USA)
2012 Massachusetts Avenue N.W.
Washington, D.C. 20036
204-293-1100

This is the oldest organization for working women. One-third of its members own small businesses. It has a resource center and its own political action committee. Offers insurance and medical benefits to members. (Members are not all women or home-business owners.)

New Ways to Work
149 Ninth Street
San Francisco, CA 94103
415-552-1000

This is a research and advocacy group for alternative work schedules, such as telecommuting, job sharing, flextime, etc. Annual membership is $25.00.

Directories

These directories and many others are available in the reference section of your library. Most are published annually.

Ayer Directory of Newspapers & Periodicals
Ayer Press
210 West Washington Square
Philadelphia, PA 19106

Broadcasting Yearbook
1735 De Sales St. N.W.
Washington, D.C. 20036
Lists contacts at radio and TV stations nationwide, by city and state.

Chase's Calendar of Annual Events
Apple Tree Press
Box 1012
Flint, MI 48501

Direct Mail List Rates and Data
Standard Rate and Data Service

Directory of Directories
Gale Research Co., Detroit
Lists over 9000 directories, rosters, and buyer's guides.

Encyclopedia of Associations
Gale Research Co.
Detroit, MI

Literary Market Place
R.R. Bowker
New York, NY

Newsletters Directory
Gale Research Co.
Detroit, MI

The Newsletter Yearbook Directory
Can be ordered by mail from:
The Newsletter Clearinghouse
44 West Market Street
P.O. Box 311
Rhinebeck, NY 12572
Lists 2000 newsletters by subject (with index). This is a good marketing tool.

Writer's Market
Writer's Digest Books
Cincinnati, OH

General Business Magazines

Business Week
P.O. Box 506
Hightstown, NJ 08520
1-800-635-1200

Entrepreneur
2311 Pontius Avenue
Los Angeles, CA 90064
213-478-0437

Forbes
60 Fifth Avenue
New York, NY 10011
212-620-2200

Fortune
Time, Inc.
541 N. Fairbanks Court
Chicago, IL 60611

Inc.
P.O. Box 54129
Boulder, CO 80322
1-800-525-0643

Home Office Computing
730 Broadway
New York, NY 10003

Nation's Business
Washington, D.C.
202-463-5650

Newsletters

Cottage Connection
National Association for the Cottage Industry
P.O. Box 14460
Chicago, IL 60614
312-472-8116

Home Based Entrepreneur Newsletter
JEB Publications
5520 S. Cornell
Chicago, IL 60637

HomeWork
The Home Business Newsletter with a Christian Perspective
Home Business Resource Center
P.O. Box 115023-233A
Carrollton, TX 75011

Homeworking Mothers
Mother's Home Business Network
P.O. Box 423
East Meadow, NY 11554
514-997-7394
Sample available for $2.00 and SASE.

National Home Business Report
Barbara Brabec Productions
P.O. Box 2138
Naperville, IL 60566
$18.00 per year, published quarterly. Sample issue is $4.00.

Newsletter for Independent Business Owners
Earl D. Brodie
465 California Street
San Francisco, CA 94104

Telecommuting Report
Electronic Services Unlimited
79 Fifth Avenue
New York, NY 10003

Telecommuting Review: The Gordon Report
Telespan Publishing Corporation
50 West Palm Street
Altadena, CA 91001

The Worksteader News
P.O. Box 820, Rancho Cordova, CA 95741
Annual subscription is $24.00

Periodicals

The Entrepreneurship Forum
The Center for Entrepreneurial Studies
Graduate School of Business Administration
New York University
90 Trinity Place
New York, NY 10006
212-285-6150

Notes

Chapter 1—A Dream That's Becoming a Trend

1. "At Home on the Job: A Change of Place for a Better Life," in *Nation's Business*, Oct. 1988, p. 36.
2. The Small Business Administration.
3. David Olmos, "New Technology Opens Door for More Workers to Stay at Home," in *Los Angeles Times*, Oct. 6, 1988.
4. "Working at Home Not Always Easy As It Sounds," in *Las Vegas Review Journal*, Mar. 22, 1988.
5. Patricia Sullivan, "Home Businesses Boom," in *The Missoulian*, Missoula, MT, Apr. 3, 1988
6. Ingrid Kindred, "Trend of the '80's: Never Leaving Home to Go to Work," in *Birmingham News*, Oct. 6, 1986.
7. "Home Offices: Not Always Heaven," *Boston Globe*, Sep. 12, 1988.
8. "Women Lead Home Business Trend," in *Olympian*, Olympia, WA, Apr. 3, 1988.
9. "The Age of the Woman Entrepreneur," in *Nation's Business*, May 1989, p. 22.
10. Ibid., p. 23.
11. "The Mommy Track: Juggling Kids and Careers in Corporate America Takes a Controversial Turn," in *Business Week*, Mar. 20, 1989, p. 127.
12. Ibid.
13. "Labor Department Lifts 45-Year Ban on Industrial Work at Home," in *Washington Post*, Nov. 5, 1988, p. A1.
14. "Giving Parents More Homework," *Family Policy*, Nov./Dec. 1988, p. 2.

15. "Escape from the Office," in *Newsweek*, Apr. 24, 1989, p. 58.
16. George and Sandra Delany, *The #1 Home Business Book* (Liberty House, 1981).

Chapter 2—The Motivation
1. Corinne M. DiBlasi, Ph.D., "Child Care: Which Way Do We Go?" in *The Texas Woman's News*, Aug. 1989, p. 4.
2. Paul and Sarah Edwards, *Working from Home: Everything You Need to Know About Living and Working Under the Same Roof* (Los Angeles: J.P. Tarcher, Inc., 1985), p. 13.
3. Roger Rickless and Udayan Gupga, "Trauma of a New Entrepreneur," in *The Wall Street Journal*, May 10, 1989.

Chapter 3—Making the Decision
1. Mary Pride, *All the Way Home* (Westchester, IL: Crossways Books/Good News, 1989), p. 188.
2. Pride, *All the Way Home*, p. 187.
3. Kindred, "Trend of the '80's."
4. Jerome Goldstein, *In Business for Yourself* (New York: Charles Scribner's Sons, 1982), p. 26.
5. "New Magazine Targets Family Businesses," in *The Wall Street Journal*, Sep. 18, 1989, p. B1.
6. Edith Flowers Kilgo, *Money in the Cookie Jar* (Grand Rapids: Baker Book House, 1980), p. 31.

Chapter 5—Home Business Profiles
1. Nicole Wise, "Successful Strategies for Part-time Work," in *Parents*, Dec. 1988. p. 76.

Chapter 6—Setting Up Your Business
1. "Zero in on Reality, in *Nation's Business*, Oct. 1988, p. 37.
2. *Legal Aspects of Small Business* (American Entrepreneurs Association, 1984), pp. 3305-12.
3. Ibid., pp. 3305-15
4. Ibid., pp. 3303-05.
5. Ibid., pp. 3305-07.
6. Kindred, "Trend of the '80's."
7. *Home Offices and Workspaces* (Menlo Park, CA: Sunset Books, Lane Publishing Co., 1986), p. 39.
8. Roger Ricklefs and Udayan Gupta, "Traumas of a New Entrepreneur," in *The Wall Street Journal*, May 10, 1989.

Chapter 8—Managing Your Business

1. Paul and Sarah Edwards, *Working from Home* (Los Angeles: J.P. Tarcher, Inc., 1987), p. 226
2. Davis Bushnell, "Home Offices Not Always Heaven," in *Boston Globe*, Sep. 12, 1988.

Chapter 9—Managing Your Time

1. Idea learned from Donna Clark Goodrich, *How to Set up and Run a Typing Service* (New York: John Wiley and Sons, 1983), p. 18.
2. Emilie Barnes, *The Creative Home Organizer* (Eugene, OR: Harvest House, 1988), p. 15.
3. Wise, "Successful Strategies for Part-time Work," p. 71.
4. "Business First, Family Second," in *The Wall Street Journal*, May 12, 1989.
5. Jim Trelease, *The Read Aloud Handbook* (New York: Penguin Books, 1982), p. 99.

Chapter 10—Managing Your Home

1. James Dobson, *Fatigue and the Homemaker* (Arcadia, CA: "Focus on the Family" booklet, 1986).
2. Luanne Shackelford and Susan White, *A Survivor's Guide to Homeschooling* (Westchester, IL: Crossway Books, 1988), p. 36.

Chapter 11—Where Do the Children Fit In?

1. "Finding Live In Help for Your Child that Is Loving, Loyal and Also Legal," in *Money*, Sep. 1989, p. 155.
2. SBA figures and the 12/15/89 broadcast of "Focus on the Family."
3. Patricia Sullivan, *The Missoulian*, Missoula MT, April 3, 1988.
4. Interview with Karen Greers, Congressional Liaison for Concerned Women of America.
5. The 12/15/89 broadcast of "Focus on the Family."
6. From a 1987 poll called *Opinion Round-Up*, from *Public Opinion*, July/Aug. 1988.
7. Interview with Bill Mattox of the Family Research Council.
8. Shackelford and White, *A Survivor's Guide to Homeschooling*, pp. 106-07.

Chapter 12—Telecommuting and Working for Other
1. "How Corporate America Takes Its Work Home," in *Modern Office Technology*, July 1989.
2. Wise, "Successful Strategies for Part-time Work," p. 76.
3. Donald C. Bacon, "Look Who's Working at Home," in *Nation's Business*, Oct. 1989, p. 30.
4. "Working at Home: Challenge for Federal Policy and Statistics," Oct. 1986, Joanne H. Pratt, ed., *Proceedings of the Symposium*, Office of Advocacy, U.S. Small Business Administration, p. 23.
5. "How Corporate America Takes Its Work Home," p. 54.
6. *Tips on Work-at-Home Schemes*, Consumer Information Series (Council of the Better Business Bureau).
7. "Home Work Grows Up," in *Democrat and Chronicle*, July 30, 1988.

Chapter 14—Keeping the Right Perspective
1. "Focus on the Family" letter by Dr. James Dobson, Oct. 1989, p. 2.

I'd Like to Hear from You!

If you would like more information concerning the Home Business Resource Center or our newsletter, *HomeWork*, please send a self-addressed stamped envelope to:

Home Business Resource Center
P.O. Box 115023-233
Carrollton, TX 75011

If you would like to share your successes, problems, tips, secrets, solutions, or experiences in working at home, please write to me. Please include permission to quote you in other writings or the newsletter *HomeWork*. Topics of particular interest:

- How are you combining your work with your family life?
- How do you work at home with young children?
- How has your life changed since you started working at home?
- How have you seen God work in your business?
- What's the most stress-producing element in your home business, and how do you cope with it?
- What do you like best about working at home?
- What do you wish you had known when you first started that you now know?
- How are you expanding your business?
- Did this book make a difference in your work at home?

Thanks and God bless,

Lindsey O'Connor

About the Author

Lindsey O'Connor is the founder of the Home Business Resource Center—a Christian organization providing resource information, encouragement, and practical advice for those who work at home.

O'Connor is also the editor of *HomeWork*, the only specialized newsletter for home-based workers written from a Christian perspective.

Other Good Harvest House Reading

SURVIVAL FOR BUSY WOMEN
Establishing Efficient Home Management
by *Emilie Barnes*

A hands-on manual for establishing a more efficient home-management program. Over 25 charts and forms can be personalized to help you organize your home.

WHERE WILL I FIND THE TIME?
Making Time Work For You
by *Sally McClung*

For most of us, the busier our lives become the less fulfilled we seem to be. *Where Will I find the Time?* offers realistic advice to everyone who wants to learn to use time more effectively. Once we learn the simple and basic principles for enjoying all the God-given dimensions of life, there's more than enough time to do the things that really matter.

Sally McClung shares her biblically-based insights for successfully prioritizing the demands of marriage, family, and work while still leaving opportunities for recreation and renewal. In her warm and personal style, McClung provides encouragement to those who struggle with life management and personal organization skills and gives practical information that can increase your effectiveness.

THE WORKING MOTHER'S GUIDE TO SANITY
by *Elsa Houtz*

Working mothers "have it all"—or do they? Written from a down-to-earth, practical perspective, *The Working Mother's Guide to Sanity* examines the most fundamental concerns and problems working mothers face.

Going beyond just identifying the problems, *The Working Mother's Guide to Sanity* provides answers, options, and solutions that work for the working mother. Filled with heartwarming examples and humorous anecdotes, Elsa Houtz shows the sometimes-funny, sometimes-trying, and always-challenging life of today's working mother.